friendly Schools PLUS

Middle Childhood

DONNA **CROSS**
SHANE **THOMPSON**
ERIN **ERCEG**

Solution Tree | Press   *a division of*

Solution Tree

Ages 8–10

Republished in the United States by Solution Tree Press

Solution Tree | Press
a division of
Solution Tree

All rights reserved.

555 North Morton Street
Bloomington, IN 47404
800.733.6786 (toll free) / 812.336.7700
FAX: 812.336.7790
email: info@solution-tree.com
solution-tree.com

Visit **go.solution-tree.com/behavior** to download the reproducibles in this book.

Printed in the United States of America

18 17 16 15 14   1 2 3 4 5

FSC
www.fsc.org
MIX
Paper from
responsible sources
FSC® C011935

Library of Congress Cataloging-in-Publication Data

Cross, Donna, 1960-
   Friendly schools plus teacher resource : middle childhood (ages 8-10) / authors, Donna Cross, Shane Thompson, Erin Erceg ; contributors, Natasha Pearce [and thirteen others].
      pages cm
   Includes bibliographical references.
   ISBN 978-1-936763-15-3 (perfect bound) 1. Bullying in schools--Prevention. 2. Bullying--Prevention. 3. School violence--Prevention. I. Thompson, Shane, 1954- II. Erceg, Erin, 1962- III. Pearce, Natasha. IV. Title.
   LB3013.3.C759 2014
   371.7'82--dc23
                        2014003797

Solution Tree
Jeffrey C. Jones, CEO
Edmund M. Ackerman, President

Solution Tree Press
President: Douglas M. Rife
Editorial Director: Lesley Bolton
Managing Production Editor: Caroline Weiss
Production Editor: Tara Perkins
Copy Editor: Sarah Payne-Mills
Proofreader: Elisabeth Abrams
Cover Designer and Compositor: Rian Anderson

Contributors
Dr. Natasha Pearce, Associate Professor Stacey Waters, Melanie Epstein, Kate Hadwen, Sarah Falconer, Helen Monks, Dr. Laura Thomas, Amy Barnes, Elizabeth Alderman, Dr. Juli Coffin, Dr. Julian Dooley, Associate Professor Margaret Hall, Dr. Yolanda Trigger, and Samuel Cecins

Published in Australia by Hawker Brownlow Education

Hawker Brownlow
EDUCATION

AUSTRALIA
ECU
EDITH COWAN UNIVERSITY

child health
Promotion Research Centre

Table of Contents

Visit **go.solution-tree.com/behavior** to download the reproducibles in this book.

Whole-School Practice

Middle Childhood

Teacher Resource
Ages 8–10

Introduction

While bullying behavior in schools is widespread and harmful, research conducted at the Child Health Promotion Research Centre (CHPRC) at Edith Cowan University and elsewhere (Baldry & Farrington, 2007; Smith, Schneider, Smith, & Ananiadou, 2004; Vreeman & Carroll, 2007) suggests bullying behavior can be reduced. The CHPRC research team's ongoing research, conducted since 1999 via eleven large empirical studies involving more than 27,000 Australian school-age students, has focused primarily on what schools can do to effectively prevent and reduce bullying behavior.

One of the most effective means to reduce bullying among young people is to enhance their social and emotional understandings and competencies in developmentally appropriate ways throughout their schooling, using a whole-school approach. Friendly Schools Plus addresses the social and emotional learning of young people, both formally through explicit classroom pedagogy and learning strategies and informally through the development of a whole-school culture, organization, and structures that reinforce and uphold these essential understandings, skills, and competencies.

The Friendly Schools Plus initiative is a strengths-based, whole-school participatory process that enables schools to determine their needs and implement current and robust evidence-based policy and practice to enhance students' social and emotional learning and reduce bullying. In particular, *Friendly Schools Plus Evidence for Practice* provides toolkits to assess and augment school staff capacity to recognize, develop, and sustain those components of a whole-school approach that support their students' unique social and emotional learning and foster the prevention of bullying behavior.

Friendly Schools Plus Initiative

A multicomponent, evidence-based whole-school initiative involving the whole school community to build social skills, create supportive environments, and significantly reduce bullying in school communities.

Friendly Schools Plus Resources

- **Planning tool for each key area**
  School teams will conduct their review of current policies and practices, identify their successes and needs, and plan their strategies and actions in each key area. The planning tool is designed for teams to record their planning for future action in each key area.
- ***Evidence for Practice* text and whole-school toolkits**
  A comprehensive book that describes research-based practice approaches that schools can implement to maximize and sustain effective social skill building and bullying prevention strategies.
- **Teacher resource books and teacher toolkits**
  Classroom teacher resource books for students ages four to fourteen and a range of online toolkits to help schools implement the recommended strategies.
- **Website—go.solution-tree.com/behavior**

What Is a Whole-School Approach?

Multicomponent whole-school initiatives involving all members of the school community are more likely to reduce bullying behavior than single-component programs, such as those involving only classroom curriculum (Farrington & Ttofi, 2009).

A whole-school approach, sometimes referred to as a Health-Promoting Schools model, recognizes that all aspects of the school community can promote (or reduce) students' health and well-being and that students' learning and their health are inextricably linked. Given young people spend much of their first seventeen years in a school environment, it is not only the focal point of their academic development but also their social development, where they make friends and develop healthy relationships. Friendly Schools Plus recognizes the importance of a whole-school approach and is organized to provide support to schools, not only through formal classroom teaching and learning, but through all aspects of the whole-school environment. To achieve sustainable behavior change that is integrated, holistic, and strategic, it is necessary to implement a whole-school approach rather than focus only on individual behavior. The essential elements of the Health-Promoting Schools approach include (International Union for Health Promotion and Education [IUHPE], n.d.):

- Healthy school policies
- The schools' physical environment
- The schools' social environment
- Individual health skills and action competencies (through formal teaching and learning)
- Community and family links
- Health services

The multicomponent Friendly Schools Plus program has integrated these components of the Health-Promoting Schools model into a comprehensive whole-school program with an emphasis on:

- Building staff capacity to implement programs to enhance students' relationships and reduce bullying
- Providing policies that shape a respectful, welcoming, and caring school environment
- Building quality relationships between school students and staff
- Maximizing the involvement of family and other members of the community
- Scaffolding students' learning of social and emotional skills, such as self-awareness, self-management, and social awareness
- Enabling students to be advocates for and to encourage positive social interpersonal development behavior online and a targeted behavior offline
- Supporting students who are frequently bullied or helping perpetrators of bullying to change their behavior

Friendly Schools Plus brings together the whole-school community to contribute to the development and ongoing maintenance of the friendly and safe culture of the school.

Section 1

The Friendly Schools Plus Implementation Model

The Friendly Schools Plus implementation model recognizes that whole-school change is sustained when evidence of good practice aligns with real-world school vision and when practice is supported with sufficient capacity (leadership, organization, competency) to drive an effective implementation process.

Layers of the Model

Evidence for Practice—Whole-School Vision—Sustainability

Whole-school change is sustained when evidence of good practice aligns with real-world school vision and practice.

The evidence for practice to reduce bullying and enhance social and emotional understandings and competencies is provided through the Friendly Schools Plus resources and professional learning. By aligning this current research evidence with the whole-school vision, schools can work toward implementing policies and practices in a coordinated and sustained manner.

Capacity for Implementation—Leadership—Organizational Support—Competencies

Whole-school change is supported with sufficient capacity (leadership, organization, competency).

The "Building Capacity" chapter in *Evidence for Practice* will assist schools in building their capacity in the areas of leadership, organizational support, and competencies to support implementation of the Friendly Schools Plus initiative.

The Friendly Schools Plus Process

The Friendly Schools Plus process helps schools review, plan, build capacity, and implement critical evidence-based actions to effectively respond to their strengths and needs in key areas, identified by the research. *Evidence for Practice* provides more information on the Friendly Schools Plus process.

Schools follow this ongoing process to assess and address these six interrelated key areas:

1. Building capacity
2. Supportive school culture
3. Proactive policies and practices
4. Key understandings and competencies
5. Protective physical environment
6. School–family–community partnerships

Schools are assisted by the Friendly Schools Plus resource *Evidence for Practice* to identify evidence-based practices to address their needs and a comprehensive planning tool to guide the planning process toward improvement.

To ensure sustainability of the Friendly Schools Plus initiative, the process must be seen as an ongoing monitoring and review process that supports the implementation of the resources over time.

Steps of the Friendly Schools Plus Process

1. Plan priorities and strategies for school policy and practice.
2. Build collective capability of all staff, through professional learning, to implement whole-school priorities and classroom actions.
3. Use the evidence-based whole-school toolkits from *Evidence for Practice* to respond to identified priorities for positive change.
4. Implement teaching and learning activities from the teacher resource books to develop the social and emotional skills of students, based on their strengths and needs.
5. Review changes in school processes, review teacher practice, and gather evidence of student outcomes to inform future practice.

Getting Started

While the steps for the Friendly Schools Plus whole-school process are numbered, there are multiple entry points for getting started. One school may have made the decision to engage in professional learning to build collective capability to improve whole-school practice. Once this decision has been made, it begins to gather evidence of current practice to inform its actions and priorities. An individual teacher within a school may have purchased and used the teacher resource book in his or her classroom with such positive results that it influences a whole-school initiative. The ultimate goal of the Friendly Schools Plus initiative is to bring together the whole-school community to contribute to the development and ongoing maintenance of the friendly and safe culture of the school.

Section 1

Chapter 1

Social and Emotional Learning

The social, emotional, cognitive, and physical aspects of a person's development are interrelated. Each influences and is influenced by the others. Consequently, it is not uncommon for students who have difficulty managing their emotions and behavior to face great challenges meeting the demands of schooling. This relationship between student behavior and academic problems is not always clear in terms of which comes first, but what is clear is that the presence of one greatly increases the risk of the other. Supporting children's emotional, social, and behavioral development thus enables students to more effectively engage in their learning.

The Friendly Schools Plus resource is designed to address three key aspects of students' school experiences shown to be related to improved social and emotional development: (1) promoting positive peer relationships, (2) promoting positive teacher-child relationships, and (3) explicit teaching related to emotions, social knowledge, and social skills. The resource aims to develop students' social and emotional competencies to enable them to recognize and control their emotions, build positive relationships, show consideration for others, make thoughtful and sensible choices, and cope successfully with difficult situations. These outcomes are developed through the following five social and emotional learning skills in this resource:

1. Self-awareness
2. Self-management
3. Social awareness
4. Relationship skills
5. Social decision making

Bullying can have a significant and negative impact on students' social and emotional development and other learning. An anxious, frightened, and withdrawn student has limited learning potential.

To reduce and ultimately prevent bullying it is important to focus on why most children and young people do not engage in bullying behavior. These individuals tend to display greater social and emotional competence than those who bully others. Children and adolescents who demonstrate social and emotional competence are also more likely to have positive relationships and social capabilities that reduce the likelihood of them being bullied. In addition, in the event that they are victimized or a bystander in a bullying incident, they are more aware of how to manage the bullying situation.

Bullying is more than an event between students who bully and students who are bullied. It is a social relationship involving group values and group standards of behavior, which means it requires consistent action across the school community to achieve positive change.

Students develop personal and social capabilities as they learn to understand themselves and others, and manage their relationships, lives, work, and learning more effectively (Brendgen, Markiewicz, Doyle, & Bukowski, 2001). The capability involves students in a range of practices including recognizing and regulating emotions, developing empathy for and understanding of others, establishing positive relationships, making responsible decisions, working effectively in teams, and handling challenging situations constructively.

Students with well-developed social and emotional skills find it easier to manage themselves, relate to others, develop resilience and a sense of self-worth, resolve conflict, engage in teamwork, and feel positive about themselves and the world around them. The development of personal and social capability is a foundation for learning and for citizenship.

What Is Social and Emotional Learning?

Social and emotional learning is the process of developing and practicing important social and emotional understandings and skills (Lagerspetz, Björkqvist, & Peltonen, 1988). These understandings and skills can be grouped into five key areas (see figure 1).

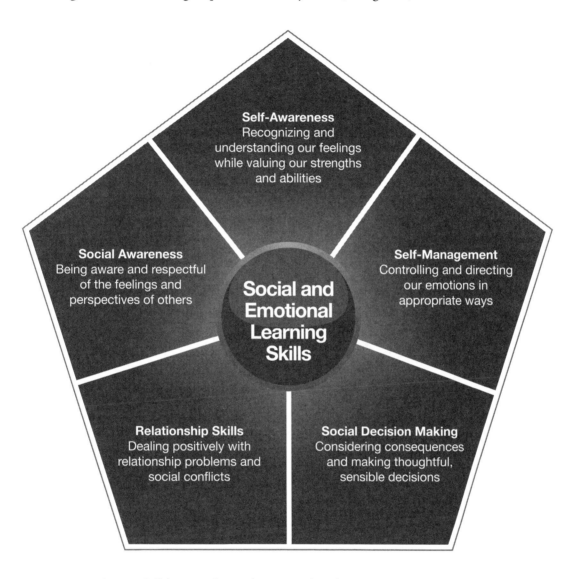

Source: Collaborative for Academic, Social, and Emotional Learning, 2011.

Figure 1: Five social and emotional learning skills.

Self-awareness skills help us recognize and understand our feelings while valuing our strengths and abilities. This involves:

- Being able to identify what we are feeling
- Understanding why we might feel a certain way
- Recognizing and having the confidence to use our strengths and abilities

Self-management skills enable us to control and direct our emotions in appropriate ways. This involves:

- Managing our emotions so they don't stop us from effectively dealing with situations and pursuing our goals
- Striving to achieve our goals despite difficulties

Social awareness skills help us to be aware and respectful of the feelings and perspectives of others. This involves:

- Recognizing what others may be feeling
- Trying to understand a situation from another's point of view
- Accepting and valuing people who are different from ourselves

Relationship skills help us to deal positively with relationship problems and other social conflicts. These skills include:

- Making friends and maintaining healthy relationships
- Dealing effectively with negative social influences and conflicts
- Seeking help if we are not able to solve a social problem ourselves

Social decision-making skills help us consider the consequences of our actions for ourselves and others and make thoughtful, sensible decisions. This involves:

- Understanding how a social situation makes us feel
- Considering the different choices we have and the positive and negative consequences of each of these choices when making a decision
- Making positive choices while considering how these choices may affect ourselves and others (Collaborative for Academic, Social, and Emotional Learning [CASEL], 2003)

Personal and social capability skills are addressed in all learning areas and at every stage of a student's schooling.

When students develop their skills in any one of these elements, it leads to greater overall personal and social capability and also enhances their skills in the other elements (Brendgen et al., 2001). In particular, the more students learn about their own emotions, values, strengths, and capacities, the more they are able to manage their own emotions and behaviors, understand others, and establish and maintain positive relationships.

Benefits of Social and Emotional Learning

Improving social and emotional skills has a positive influence on children and adolescents' attitudes, behaviors, and performance (Lagerspetz et al., 1988). A review of 317 studies involving over 300,000 children and adolescents found that social and emotional learning programs were beneficial for children and young people aged five through eighteen from urban and rural communities with or without behavioral or emotional problems (Crick & Bigbee, 1998). Social and emotional learning improved participants' social and emotional skills, coping skills, and resistance to negative peer pressure; resulted in more positive attitudes toward themselves, others, and their schools; improved social behaviors and cooperation with others; decreased risky, antisocial, and aggressive behaviors; and decreased emotional problems, including anxiety and depression (Crick & Bigbee, 1998).

Other research also suggests that social and emotional learning programs improve health outcomes for young people, including a decreased risk of tobacco, alcohol, and illicit substance use problems; mental health problems and suicide; and sexually transmitted diseases (Lagerspetz et al., 1988).

Social and emotional learning programs can also improve academic success, with students demonstrating improved grades and test scores, more positive attitudes toward school, and better school attendance, as well as heightened trust and respect for teachers, improved management of school-related stress, improved participation in class, and fewer suspensions (Lagerspetz et al., 1988; Smith, Talamelli, Cowie, Naylor, & Chauhan, 2004).

These programs also show evidence of long-term effectiveness, especially if social skills are developed and consolidated across several years (Smith, Talamelli, et al., 2004). Importantly, the positive effects of social and emotional learning can extend beyond the individual with improvements in students' social and emotional skills likely to have a positive influence on their schools, families, and broader communities (Galen & Underwood, 1997).

Social and Emotional Learning in the School Curriculum

To make ethical, constructive choices about personal and social behavior, children and young people need to show understanding about themselves and be able to take the perspective of and empathize with others. Being empathetic means being able to identify with, understand, and care about how another person feels in a certain situation. This is especially important for students to reduce the bullying perpetration and to help those who are victimized.

Many students have not yet had the life experiences to enable them to directly understand or relate to what another person might think, feel, or believe in a certain situation. Students benefit from the explicit teaching and learning activities that interrogate the different perspectives of individuals and groups involved in the social context and the decision-making processes they may apply to different social situations, such as preventing or responding to bullying.

The Friendly Schools Plus resource uses stories and literature, cooperative games, role plays, problem solving, and reflective activities to encourage students to identify and understand their emotions, consider the perspectives of others, negotiate tricky situations, and make well-reasoned decisions (Dooley, Cross, Hearn, & Treyvaud, 2009). This comprehensive resource provides sequential, interactive, and engaging learning activities to explicitly build social and emotional competencies in students that are important for each major developmental stage from primary to secondary school.

Social and Emotional Learning by Developmental Level

The most effective learning programs are those that integrate social learning into the curriculum, specifically targeting and building on social and emotional skills over time, from preschool to high school. While there may be considerable variation in children's and adolescents' social and emotional skills, broad patterns are associated with early and middle childhood as well as early and middle adolescence (Galen & Underwood, 1997; Rigby, 1996).

Early Childhood

From ages four to eight children increasingly begin to use reason to understand the world, consider the needs of others, and take responsibility for their actions. Developing confidence in their abilities and establishing healthy relationships are important during this stage (Crick & Dodge, 1994; Fontaine & Dodge, 2006).

Table 1: Early Childhood Social and Emotional Skills				
Self-Awareness	**Self-Management**	**Social Awareness**	**Relationship Skills**	**Social Decision Making**
Can identify personal: • Likes and dislikes • Needs and wants • Strengths and challenges	Can identify personal: • Emotions • Appropriate classroom behavior Can control impulsive behavior	Can use listening skills to identify feelings of others Can describe: • Ways people are similar and different • Positive qualities in others • Different ways people may experience situations	Can identify: • Ways to work and play well with others • Common problems and conflicts of peers • Approaches to positively deal with conflicts Can demonstrate appropriate social and class behavior	Can explain why aggression toward others is wrong Can identify: • Safe social behaviors • Range of decisions to make at school • Roles in classroom and contribute to these Can make positive decisions with peers

Source: CASEL, 2011.

Middle Childhood

From ages eight to eleven children become increasingly independent but also more aware of social situations and relationships. Feeling like part of a group and receiving social acceptance are particularly important at this time (Crick & Dodge, 1994; Dodge & Coie, 1987).

Table 2: Middle Childhood Social and Emotional Skills				
Self-Awareness	**Self-Management**	**Social Awareness**	**Relationship Skills**	**Social Decision Making**
Can describe: • Personal skills and interests they wish to develop • How family members and others can support positive behavior	Can describe: • Range of emotions and situations that cause them Can demonstrate ways to express emotions in socially acceptable manner Can take steps toward and monitor goal achievement	Can recognize social cues that indicate how others may feel Can describe feelings and views expressed by others Can identify: • Differences and similarities between groups • Contributions of different groups and how to work with these groups	Can describe: • How to make and keep friends • How to work effectively in groups • Causes and consequences of conflicts Can apply constructive approaches to resolving conflicts	Can demonstrate: • Ability to respect rights of self and others • Knowledge of how social norms affect decision making and behavior Can apply the steps of decision making and identify and evaluate consequences Can identify and contribute to roles to help in the community

Source: CASEL, 2011.

Early Adolescence

From ages eleven to thirteen young adolescents have improved self-control and self-reliance. They often have strong concerns about fitting in and physical appearance. Social and emotional skills have become more advanced, with young adolescents better able to analyze consequences and negotiate conflicts and interpersonal problems. Young people are also very concerned about making and keeping friends, including opposite-sex friendships. They also have a greater need for independence from adults, often resisting the influence of parents and teachers and using peers to determine behavioral norms (Crick & Dodge, 1994; Dodge, Lochman, Harnish, Bates, & Pettit, 1997).

Table 3: Early Adolescence Social and Emotional Skills				
Self-Awareness	**Self-Management**	**Social Awareness**	**Relationship Skills**	**Social Decision Making**
Can analyze how: • Personal qualities influence choices and success • Using available supports can improve success	Can analyze factors to enhance or inhibit performance Can apply strategies to manage stress and improve performance Can set a short-term goal and plan to achieve it and analyze success or otherwise	Can predict others' feelings and perspectives Can analyze how personal behavior may affect others Can explain how cultural differences can increase vulnerability to bullying and identify ways to reduce this Can analyze the effects of taking action to oppose bullying	Can analyze ways to build positive relationships with others Can demonstrate cooperation and teamwork to improve group processes Can evaluate strategies for preventing and resolving relationship problems Can identify negative peer influence and determine ways to respond to it	Can evaluate how values such as honesty and respect help to take into account the needs of others when making decisions Can explain the reasons for rules Can evaluate strategies to respond to negative peer influence Can evaluate their contribution to addressing needs in school and in the community

Source: CASEL, 2011.

Middle Adolescence

From ages thirteen to fifteen adolescents increasingly learn to balance freedom and fun with responsibilities, and individuality with peer influence. They value respect from others and independence from adults, and become more concerned with pursuing their own goals (Crick & Dodge, 1994; Vitiello & Stoff, 1997).

Table 4: Middle Adolescence Social and Emotional Skills				
Self-Awareness	**Self-Management**	**Social Awareness**	**Relationship Skills**	**Social Decision Making**
Can analyze how positive adult role models and other supports contribute to success Can set priorities to build strengths and determine areas for improvement	Can analyze how thoughts and emotions affect decision making and responsible behavior Can monitor and find ways to develop more positive attitudes Can analyze and apply strategies to overcome barriers to achieving goals	Can analyze similarities and differences between their own and others' perspectives Can use interpersonal skills to understand others' perspectives and feelings Can examine and respond to negative stereotypes and prejudice Can demonstrate respect for individuals from other social and cultural groups	Can evaluate their contribution to groups in which they are a leader or member Can evaluate the impact of requesting or providing support to others Can analyze actions they can take to help resolve conflicts as an individual or in a group	Can demonstrate taking personal responsibility for ethical decisions Can evaluate how social norms and expectations influence their decision making Can apply decision-making skills to establish responsible social relationships Can evaluate their ability to anticipate the consequences of social decisions Can plan, implement, and evaluate their participation in activities to improve the school and local community

Source: CASEL, 2011.

Each developmental level as described in the tables is associated with the need for increasingly refined social and emotional learning. To meet this need, the Friendly Schools Plus resource gradually increases the complexity of the age-appropriate activities provided for each age group. This allows students to build on and refine their social and emotional skills over time.

Chapter 2

Bullying—Evidence Before Action

This chapter presents an overview of the research evidence describing the nature, causes, correlates, and impacts of bullying behaviors, as well as strategies for managing bullying in the classroom. Importantly, this chapter will help to ensure a consistent and accurate understanding of what is meant by the term *bullying*, its causes, outcomes, and the consequences.

Defining and Measuring Bullying

What Is Bullying?

The definition used by most researchers today is:

> Bullying is a repeated behavior; that may be physical, verbal, and/or psychological; where there is intent to cause fear, distress, or harm to another; that is conducted by a more powerful individual or group; against a less powerful individual or group of individuals who are unable to stop this from happening. (Olweus, 1996)

The key elements of a bullying incident include both a perpetrator's and target's perspective—the perpetrator has more perceived power, he or she repeats the behavior and with intention, while the target feels the bullying is unprovoked or unjustifiable and he or she is not able to stop the behavior from happening. If these elements are not present, using this definition, the behavior would be considered an aggressive act and not an incident of bullying.

When talking with young people about bullying, it is more understandable to describe bullying as a series of descriptive behaviors, rather than one broad term that has many negative connotations, especially when discussing cyberbullying. The behaviors commonly used to describe bullying include being repeatedly:

- Ignored or left out on purpose
- Made fun of or teased in a mean and hurtful way
- Made to feel afraid of getting hurt
- Stared at with mean looks or gestures
- Embarrassed by nasty stories or rumors spread about you
- Forced to do things you don't want to
- Hit, kicked, or pushed around

There has been much discussion about cyberbullying and how it should best be defined. Proposed definitions range from a focus on only behavior to only technology. Following six years of assessing, evaluating, and addressing cyberbullying in schools, the Child Health Promotion Research Centre (CHPRC, 2010) defines cyberbullying as follows:

> Cyberbullying is when a group or an individual use information and communication technologies (ICT) to intentionally harm a person over time, who cannot easily stop this bullying from continuing.

The most important aspect of this definition is that it is not focused on ICT but stipulates that cyberbullying is bullying via ICT. That is, it is about the behavior, not about the technology.

What Is *Not* Bullying?

Given the complex definition of bullying, it is important to also consider what behaviors are not bullying. One example of what is not considered bullying is a fight between two equally matched students. Friendly teasing is also not considered bullying. These examples seem very clear from a perpetrator's perspective but are less so from the perspective of the target or student who is being victimized. Sometimes alleged perpetrators report they were only joking when accused of bullying. The accurate identification of "true" bullying cases is even more complicated when the bullying occurs online or by mobile phone.

Imagine the following: *Tracey is a ninth grader who comes to see you because she is being bullied. She tells you that students in her class are saying nasty things and posting hurtful pictures of her on the Internet. You find out that it was Rachel, another ninth grader. Rachel tells you that she only posted one picture and it was just meant to be a joke.*

If bullying is defined as a repeated act (that is, the definition is from Rachel's perspective), then one act, such as posting an embarrassing picture, may not be considered bullying. However, from the target's perspective (Tracey's), this act may very well be bullying given the picture is available online and can be viewed repeatedly by her and others. To address this definitional challenge, many schools refer to these cyber-related behaviors in their policies, for example, as *cyber aggression* without trying to determine if they are bullying or not, while acknowledging that these behaviors are unacceptable.

Are There Different Types of Bullying Behaviors?

A large variety of behaviors can be used to bully others. For example, bullying can be *physical, verbal, social, relational,* delivered through noncyber (for example, face-to-face) or cyber means (for example, via phone texting). *Physical bullying* includes behaviors such as hitting, kicking, pushing, tripping, and spitting (Craig, Pepler, & Blais, 2007; Smokowski & Holland, 2005). These overt behaviors (easily seen) are typically more common in boys, and it is relatively easy to identify both the perpetrator and the target (Smokowski & Holland, 2005). *Verbal bullying* involves using words to hurt or humiliate others and includes behaviors such as threats, hurtful teasing, and insults (Craig et al., 2007; Smokowski & Holland, 2005). These behaviors are less easy to detect and likely to be a component of nearly all bullying interactions (Smokowski & Holland, 2005).

Covert bullying refers to behaviors that are hard to see (Cross et al., 2009) and include indirect, relational, and social forms of bullying. The term *indirect aggression* was introduced in the late 1980s to describe aggressive and bullying behaviors that were not easily noticeable and where the perpetrator's identity was largely concealed (Lagerspetz et al., 1988). Indirect aggression could, in fact, include very overt acts that are carried out at times when the likelihood of being discovered is minimal (for example, engaging in property damage at night). In addition, indirect aggression could consist of behaviors enacted through a third party so that there is no direct contact between the perpetrator and the target.

Crick and colleagues conceptualized *relational aggression* as including behaviors that were intended to harm others by damaging relationships or feelings of social acceptance, friendship, or inclusion in peer groups (CASEL, 2011). Thus, relational aggression can comprise many different behaviors, such as playing practical jokes and embarrassing a person, imitating people behind their backs, breaking secrets, being critical, spreading hurtful rumors, sending abusive notes, whispering, or maliciously excluding them (Crick & Bigbee, 1998; Smith, Talamelli, et al., 2004).

Social bullying (or social aggression) refers to a broad behavioral concept encompassing both indirect and relational aggression that includes behaviors intended to damage or harm a person's social status or self-esteem (or both). These behaviors may include verbal rejection, negative facial expressions or body movements, or more indirect forms such as slanderous rumors or social exclusion (Galen & Underwood, 1997).

Of course, *cyberbullying* behaviors are different again given the reliance on ICT as a medium to bully. The measurement of cyberbullying behaviors represents a challenge for researchers, schools, and the community alike because the dynamic environment of the Internet (and mobile phones) means the strategies used to cyberbully others can change. The Australian Covert Bullying Prevalence Study (Cross et al., 2009) revealed some very interesting patterns of cyberbullying behaviors which highlighted, for example, the developmental nature of strategies used to victimize others.

Given the uptake of social networking and the use of social media in later adolescence, it is not surprising that social media is used as one of the most common ways to cyberbully young people (Dooley et al., 2009). In contrast, relatively more young children use email than social networking compared to the number of older teenagers who use email versus social networking (Dooley et al., 2009). However, this is likely to change as interest in and uptake of social media become more popular. Interestingly, significant differences were found in bullying behaviors between students who were the same age but located in primary versus secondary schools (Dooley et al., 2009). This is most likely related to social changes that occur when young people transition from primary to secondary school.

Table 5: Examples of Bullying Behavior		
	Direct	**Indirect**
Physical	• Hitting, slapping, punching • Kicking • Pushing • Spitting, biting • Pinching, scratching • Throwing things	• Getting another person to harm someone
Verbal	• Mean and hurtful name-calling • Hurtful teasing • Demanding money or possessions • Forcing another to do homework or commit offenses such as stealing	• Spreading nasty rumors • Trying to get other students to not like someone
Nonverbal	• Threatening or obscene gestures	• Deliberate exclusion from a group or activity • Removing and hiding or damaging others' belongings
Cyber	• Filming someone without his or her knowledge or permission • Updating someone else's social networking status without his or her permission • Pretending to be someone else on the phone	• Telling someone else the words you want him or her to type as a message • Explaining to someone how to engage in bullying via a website the other person may not be familiar with • Watching someone engaging in cyberbullying and not trying to stop the bullying

Source: Rigby, 1996.

Why Do Most Students *Not* Bully?

Although bullying situations are experienced in most schools at some time, bullying does not occur among all young people all the time. In fact, most students do not bully others. In general, young people who have developed good social and emotional skills, have positive friends, and have supportive environments at home, at school, and in the community are unlikely to bully others.

Nevertheless, some students may use bullying behaviors for a variety of reasons.

Why Do Some Students Bully?

Students use bullying behaviors for a variety of reasons. These are mainly personal in nature and typically have little to do with the person who is the target of the bullying. Some of the reasons students bully others include:

- To get what they want
- To be popular and admired
- Because they are afraid of being the one left out
- Jealousy of others
- It seems like fun
- Out of boredom
- It has worked for them before
- They enjoy the power
- They see it as their role (for example, leader)
- Their significant role models use bullying behaviors

While these reasons help to explain why students bully others, they don't explain how and why the behavior first starts. Some of the factors associated with the development of bullying in children and young people include:

- Experiencing aggressive behavior at home and elsewhere
- Being harshly, physically punished at home
- Spending time with peers who bully
- Insufficient adult supervision
- Bullying gives them the social rewards they seek
- Bullying others to prevent being bullied
- Getting attention

What Are the Effects of Bullying Behaviors?

Bullying behaviors have negative consequences for young people's physical health, mental health, social development, and academic achievement. These consequences can affect all those who are involved in bullying situations, including those who are bullied, those who bully others, and those who witness bullying.

Young people who are bullied are at increased risk of injury and poor physical health, as well as mental health problems including anxiety and depression, eating disorders, deliberate self-harm, low self-esteem, and suicidal thoughts or behavior. These students may often experience social rejection and exclusion, have difficulty making friends and maintaining good relationships with peers, and report increased loneliness. Students who are bullied are also more likely to dislike and want to avoid school and have higher rates of absenteeism. They have greater difficulty concentrating and completing work in class, and their academic achievement is often lower in comparison to other students.

Students who bully others also have decreased health and well-being. These students are at increased risk of anxiety, depression, and suicide, physical injury, and substance use and binge drinking. They are at increased risk of delinquent behaviors including arson, running away, carrying weapons, and committing violent acts. Students who bully others also tend to dislike school and have decreased academic achievement. They tend to have poorer job prospects in adulthood.

Students who are both bullied and bully others (commonly called *bully/victims*) experience many of these negative consequences, often more severely than students who are only bullied or who only bully others.

How Can Bullying Be Addressed?

Friendly Schools Plus Evidence for Practice: Whole-School Strategies to Enhance Students' Social Skills and Reduce Bullying in Schools is the research-based text that informed the development of the *Friendly Schools Plus* teacher resource books.

Extracts from *Evidence for Practice* are included in this text to provide strategies for good practice that can be implemented across the whole school in the following areas:

- Effective classroom practice and environment
- Positive peer group influence
- Physical attributes of the school
- Supportive school facilities and activities
- Strengthening family links

The information that follows will develop a base of shared understandings to develop collective responsibility for proactively addressing bullying issues. For more information regarding these strategies, refer to *Evidence for Practice*.

Chapter 3

Effective Classroom Practice and Environment

An inclusive, trusting classroom environment will help students build care and empathy for others and provide cooperative and productive learning opportunities. Effective management of the classroom by teachers includes providing an environment in which students can be:

- Focused
- Attentive
- Conscientious
- Actively engaged
- Connected to teachers and fellow students (Emmer & Stough, 2001; McNeely, Nonnemaker, & Blum, 2002)

Promoting a normative culture of disapproval of bullying within the classroom and using social skill building and bullying prevention and response strategies that are consistent with the school's positive approach maintain a safe and supportive school.

Strategies for Good Practice: Effective Classroom Practice and Environment

1. Students participate actively in the development of classroom rules about bullying behaviors, which are demonstrated consistently with the school policy.
2. Teachers have an understanding of their responsibility as behavioral role models.
3. Teachers use positive behavior expectation strategies in the classroom to promote effective learning.
4. Teachers use their classroom, curriculum, and knowledge of students to help those who are bullied and those who engage in bullying.
5. Behavior support strategies are implemented to help students develop self-control and responsibility.
6. A variety of group activities and structures are used to facilitate positive decision making about bullying situations.
7. Teachers engage students in cooperative learning methods and activities.

 Students participate actively in the development of classroom rules about bullying behaviors, which are demonstrated consistently with the school policy.

Classroom rules—based on the school's behavioral policies and written as clear statements of expected behaviors—reflect the culture the school aims to promote. Student involvement in the development of these rules enhances their compliance, responsibility, and ownership. In secondary schools, this consultation with students may occur through the student leadership council and tutor group meetings. Learning activities can provide opportunities for identifying and practicing specific behaviors to support implementation of classroom rules.

Students may need help to encourage the reporting of bullying. The following statements may help students.

Asking for Help Versus Tattling

Asking for help is when someone feels the situation is out of his or her control and he or she is unable to deal with it alone and needs help.

"Tattling" is when a person tries to get attention or to get someone else into trouble.

Asking for help for yourself or others is always OK.

Teachers have an understanding of their responsibility as behavioral role models.

Teachers are responsible for ensuring the online and offline social behaviors they model encompass the core values promoted within the school community. When teachers model pro-social skills such as respect, compassion, and negotiation, students learn to use these skills in their own social situations. All staff need to have a strong understanding of expected staff and student behaviors, particularly with the growth in popularity of online social networking sites, as discussed in *Evidence for Practice*. Further, Proactive Policies and Practices toolkit 4.5 in *Evidence for Practice* discusses opportunities for promotion of these understandings and competencies through the school's behavior expectations policy.

 Teachers use positive behavior expectation strategies in the classroom to promote effective learning.

Staff who successfully develop positive behavioral expectations for students:

- Use positive recognition as a means of promoting the pro-social behavior of students
- Help students who engage in bullying behavior develop more appropriate modes of behaving
- Provide positive ways of using student leadership and peer support skills
- Encourage commitment to the values of trust and respect and a shared understanding of social rules and procedures

 Teachers use their classroom, curriculum, and knowledge of students to help those who are bullied and those who engage in bullying.

Using strategic seating and grouping arrangements in the classroom can positively impact cohesion, academic satisfaction, and bullying behaviors. This may be particularly useful in secondary environments and at times of transition, when students choose their own groups and seating arrangements and may therefore be more vulnerable to exclusionary practices. Teachers can use their knowledge of the class's social relationships to group students in ways that will enhance constructive interaction, including:

- Set role grouping
- Vertical grouping
- Interest grouping
- Expertise grouping
- Experience grouping

Embedding bullying prevention and positive technology use content in the curriculum enables the development of a shared understanding of classroom and social expectations, which support those who are bullied and those who bully others. Key Understandings and Competencies toolkit 5.1 in *Evidence for Practice* discusses the Friendly Schools Plus teaching and learning materials in more detail.

 Behavior support strategies are implemented to help students develop self-control and responsibility.

School staff can help to build students' capacity to manage their own emotions and behaviors, identify social goals and how to achieve them in a positive way, and view social experiences positively.

These behavioral support strategies are best tailored to meet the strengths and needs of the school community.

Supportive School Culture toolkit 3.3 in *Evidence for Practice* outlines peer support strategies that can be used to help students develop appropriate behavior when engaging with other students. In addition, the development of assertive social skills, as discussed in Supportive School Culture toolkit 3.5, enables students to communicate more clearly and effectively with others.

 A variety of group activities and structures are used to facilitate positive decision making about bullying situations.

To make informed decisions about bullying situations, students need to be provided with the opportunity to learn and practice decision-making skills. Providing students with a social decision-making framework allows a range of alternatives to be considered and explored before a decision is made. Students need to be encouraged to recognize their values and feelings toward the consequences of the decisions they make. Providing regular opportunities to practice decision making facilitates students' ability to use this process in bullying situations.

A group decision-making model including the following five components can be beneficial.

1. State the problem.
2. Gather information.
3. Examine the choices.
4. Consider the positive and negative consequences.
5. Decide, execute, and evaluate.

Decision making is a key theme promoted throughout the Friendly Schools Plus teaching and learning materials described in Key Understandings and Competencies toolkit 5.1.

 Teachers engage students in cooperative learning methods and activities.

Schools that implement a cooperative curriculum encourage a shared understanding of social rules and procedures and enable positive outcomes relating to group interaction. These activities promote honest communication, understanding differing perspectives, and students' positive sense of self and concern for others.

Cooperative skills to promote in the classroom include:

- Respecting other people's opinions
- Sharing
- Including others
- Negotiating
- Solving and responding to fights and arguments
- Suggesting and persuading (versus bossing)
- Making group decisions

These skills can further be reinforced by parents and can be promoted through school newsletters (see Supportive School Culture toolkit 3.1), school assemblies (see Supportive School Culture toolkit 3.2), and family communication sheets (see School–Family–Community Partnerships toolkits 7.2 and 7.3).

Chapter 4

Positive Peer Group Influence

Positive peer group influence includes the authentic participation of students in the planning, implementation, and evaluation of school actions, particularly those to reduce bullying. This can lead to increased student ownership and support and greater respect for systems and structures. Recognizing, valuing, and encouraging student participation fosters collaboration between students and staff, assists in ensuring school practices are relevant and helpful, and lets students know their voices are heard. Schools can foster positive peer group influence by:

- Offering education targeting specific strategies to provide support for students being bullied
- Encouraging peer intervention in bullying (such as the responsibilities of bystanders)
- Encouraging students to withhold the social rewards that may maintain bullying
- Promoting positive peer group influence and group norms that actively discourage bullying

Strategies for Good Practice: Positive Peer Group Influence

1. Students are valued as active participants in the development of school plans, policy, and practice to reduce bullying.
2. Opportunities for students to voice their opinions are valued, encouraged, and incorporated into school planning and activities.
3. Peer group actions to reduce bullying (such as positive bystander behaviors) are encouraged and commended at the whole-school level.
4. Support and empathy for students being bullied are encouraged.

 Students are valued as active participants in the development of school plans, policy, and practice to reduce bullying.

Students can be actively engaged in policy development by:

- Identifying how they would like to see staff respond to bullying situations
- Identifying where bullying occurs (potential hot spots)
- Identifying safer zones
- Reviewing the policy
- Identifying ways to distribute the policy
- Assisting with the design of the policy to make it engaging for students

The finished policy needs to be understood and accessible to all school community members. *Evidence for Practice* chapter 4, "Proactive Policies and Practices," discusses proactive policy development and implementation for the whole-school community. In particular, Proactive Policies and Practices toolkit 4.5 provides suggestions for reviewing the school's behavior expectation policies, including how to involve students in this process.

 Opportunities for students to voice their opinions are valued, encouraged, and incorporated into school planning and activities.

Students have excellent ideas on how to promote positive behavior across the school community and solve problems. When the focus is on students taking action and accepting responsibility for the outcome, results can be more powerful and meaningful. While each school will have a unique way of engaging students, the following may provide some initial ideas:

- Student councils
- Student trainers for parents and younger students (especially in ICT)
- Students as researchers
- Students as interviewers
- Student events managers
- Student tour guides
- Students involved in policy writing
- Students leading learning (input into inspiring programs offered at the school)
- Student break time leaders (leading activities offered in break times)

It is not recommended that students are selected to play a formal role in resolving bullying situations (for example, peer mentoring). Students are well placed to encourage positive social behavior and contribute to strategies that provide a supportive environment for students, such as online and offline procedures that make it easy for students to report bullying (see Supportive School Culture toolkit 3.3 for a discussion of peer support strategies).

 Peer group actions to reduce bullying (such as positive bystander behaviors) are encouraged and commended at the whole-school level.

Bullying behavior in the school usually takes place in the presence of other students (peers). Although many students do not agree with bullying, most do not intervene to stop the bullying, but instead act in ways that enable and maintain bullying (Craig, Pepler, & Atlas, 2000; O'Connell, Pepler, & Craig, 1999). It is important that the onus for intervening in bullying incidents is not left to students alone, but rather, peer intervention efforts are viewed as complimentary to a whole-school approach to tackling bullying. Ensuring staff respond consistently increases students' ability and willingness to intervene as they know they will be supported.

Teachers and school administrators who model consistent responses to bullying behavior will see increased levels of peer intervention efforts. When students are mobilized to take action against bullying, they must feel secure that teachers understand their need to stay safe. For some students, in both primary and secondary schools, this means ensuring the information they share will not cause them to lose status in their peer group.

Leaders who provide opportunities for their staff to understand the reasons students may or may not be willing to intervene as bystanders increase their school's capacity to actively engage more students in positive bystander responses. Strategies for engaging bystanders are described in Supportive School Culture toolkit 3.4.

 Support and empathy for students being bullied are encouraged.

To respect how another student is feeling and respond in a positive and supportive way are key to showing kindness, compassion, and friendship and are integral to a supportive school culture. It can be hard to understand another person's experience of a situation, especially if we have not experienced it ourselves. It is possible, however, to respect other people's feelings and opinions.

Commonly recognized means of exhibiting respect in a school include:

- Listening carefully
- Offering encouragement
- Being nonjudgmental
- Acknowledging experiences
- Allowing for privacy and personal space in times of distress
- Asking students to define what respect and support mean for them—what they look like, feel like, and sound like

Chapter 5

Physical Attributes of the School

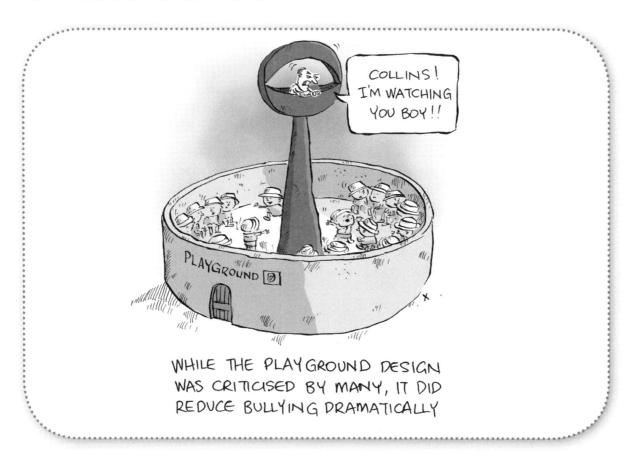

WHILE THE PLAYGROUND DESIGN WAS CRITICISED BY MANY, IT DID REDUCE BULLYING DRAMATICALLY

An attractive and well-maintained school environment suggests to students their school values comfortable, friendly, and well-maintained surroundings. This can also impact students' feelings of safety and connection to members of their school community. Well-designed, planned, and constructed school environments are another learning environment that can improve social relationships among students and staff and promote positive attitudes. These environments also help reduce absenteeism and boost students' and staff self-esteem. All members of the school community can participate in efforts to modify their physical environment and also contribute to school connectedness by creating warm environments where staff and students feel their opinions and ideas are valued.

Schools can increase students' feelings of ownership, pride, and responsibility in maintaining their surroundings when they:

- Provide adequate space for activities during break times
- Organize seating structures to facilitate positive social interactions
- Conduct regular assessments of the school's physical environment
- Use these assessments to inform modifications
- Include students in the decision-making process

Strategies for Good Practice: Physical Attributes of the School

1. An assessment of the school's physical environment is conducted annually.
2. An attractive, friendly school environment is maintained.
3. The main entrance is well defined and welcoming to all members of the school community.

 An assessment of the school's physical environment is conducted annually.

During free play or recess, students need a variety of play areas that are well supervised and areas they can go to if they feel unsafe or uncomfortable. The identification by students of areas where they feel less safe, and clear guidelines or policies regarding the use of these areas, will help schools to reduce the potential for bullying behavior.

An assessment of the school's physical environment can involve mapping and reviewing aspects of the environment that may enable or prevent bullying. For example, mapping these areas will allow the school to see overlapping supervision areas or areas that lack adequate supervision or safety. It is also important to consider access to facilities and equipment for all age groups.

The following are suggestions for reviewing the school's physical environment as well as procedures for reporting and recording school bullying incidents followed by questions that will help to evaluate the effectiveness of these methods.

Step 1: Mapping Your School's Physical Environment

Use a map of the school to identify:

- Outdoor and recreation areas (by grade level if applicable)
- Outdoor equipment
- Out-of-bounds areas
- Safest areas
- Supervision areas, including the number of staff assigned to each area, and time-out areas

An example of a student-friendly school map can be found in Protective Physical Environment toolkit 6.1, or readers may use existing maps of the school.

Step 2: Mapping Locations of Bullying Incidents

Using the map of the school's physical environment delineating the safest areas, supervision areas, boundaries, and so on, highlight the hot spots where bullying incidents are typically occurring using the school's records of bullying incidents. Consider supplying rough maps of the school (inside and out) or take photographs around the school, and ask students to highlight the places they believe bullying (including cyberbullying) takes place or where they feel unsafe. In a secondary setting, students can also be challenged by seeking submissions from students detailing their safer schoolyard designs, rationale, and recommendations. Compare these hot spots with the supervision boundaries, access to activities or equipment, and out-of-bounds areas.

Step 3: Review of the Physical Environment Map

Discuss the results of schoolyard mapping with all staff. Using the Protective Physical Environment toolkit 6.2 planning sheet, consider the potential problem areas and plan strategies for action. Consider the following questions while completing this review.

- **Are adequate areas provided for all students to play or spend time together?**
  Are there grassed, shaded, covered, and paved areas; sports and other equipment; and open spaces for students of all ages?
- **Are areas identified where students should not be spending time?**
  Are there areas that are unsafe, where supervision is limited, or where students are blocked from the view of duty teachers?
- **Are there some areas that are currently considered out-of-bounds that could become safer areas for students to spend time?**
  For example, the library provides a nonthreatening environment that is often seen by students as an area that has more teacher supervision and can, therefore, be safer from bullying than the schoolyard.
- **Are areas available during break times with higher levels of teacher supervision for students who may feel unsafe?**
  Areas supervised by empathic staff members should be provided within all school environments to enable students to seek refuge if they are bullied during break times.
- **Are time-out areas provided for students who display antisocial or bullying behaviors?**
  Asking students who are engaging in bullying or other antisocial behavior to take some time out from the situation provides an opportunity for them to cool down and reflect on their actions.
- **Are all outside areas supervised by teachers?**
  Recording the location and the types of activities students are engaging in allows the school to provide adequate levels of supervision.
- **Do all staff perceive it is their role to intervene in bullying incidents in the schoolyard?**
  Some staff can be reluctant to intervene in a bullying incident. Ensure staff are able to identify a bullying incident and respond in accordance with school procedures set out in school behavior policies.

Top tips for school improvement:

- Improve the coverage of teacher supervision of outdoor areas and bullying hot spots.
- Create safer areas for students to spend time during class breaks to avoid being bullied.
- Establish a time-out area for students who have behaved inappropriately to spend time during class breaks.
- Provide staff with skills and confidence to identify and respond effectively in bullying incidents.
- Create out-of-bounds areas in locations where teacher supervision is limited or bullying is prevalent.

An attractive, friendly school environment is maintained.

Well-maintained, attractive school environments can have a positive impact on student attitude, behavior, motivation, and connectedness.

Some ways to make schools more attractive include:

- Removing graffiti as quickly as possible
- Providing forms for reporting school maintenance and improvements that are needed around the school and acting on them
- Regularly checking cleanliness and temperatures of all learning areas
- Creating garden beds using a variety of different plants
- Displaying student artwork and photographs around the school
- Acknowledging at assemblies and in newsletters or e-letters the commitment of the school community to maintaining school buildings and grounds

 The main entrance is well defined and welcoming to all members of the school community.

A school whose main entrance is easy to locate and is warm and welcoming sends a strong and positive message to students and their families. It also promotes the school as a place committed to creating positive learning experiences. Many large companies and corporations invest significant amounts of money into how their main entrance looks to elicit a positive first impression from their customers and clients. While schools do not need to invest significant funding, a coat of paint, cultural symbols such as regional art, and student work can leave a lasting impression on parents, students, and visitors to the school.

Chapter 6
....

Supportive School Facilities and Activities

Adequate facilities, such as seating within the school, help to ensure students enjoy their break times in constructive and engaging ways and participate in positive social interactions. Supportive school activities, such as semi-structured physical and nonphysical games, provide students with opportunities to develop an understanding of social rules. School leaders who expect appropriate behavior to be modeled at all times by all staff will notice an improvement in behaviors and attitudes of students. Schools that provide opportunities for responsible technology use demonstrate to students an awareness of the important role of technology in their lives and the potential benefits this can give to their social and educational development.

Strategies for Good Practice: Supportive School Facilities and Activities

1. Developmentally appropriate, competitive, and noncompetitive games and activities are provided during break times to assist students' skill development and understanding of social rules.
2. Students are encouraged to help younger students join in activities during break times.
3. Students are taught how to positively resolve conflicts and disagreements in games without requiring adult intervention.
4. Supervised opportunities are provided for students to positively use technology for academic and social purposes.
5. Outdoor areas, out-of-bounds areas, and "safer" areas are clearly identified to students, and students are encouraged to spend time in areas where adequate supervision is provided.
6. Health and other student support services are located in areas that encourage student access.
7. Competent supervision is provided by school staff.
8. Targeted professional learning is provided for duty teachers to identify and respond appropriately and effectively to bullying situations.

 Developmentally appropriate, competitive, and noncompetitive games and activities are provided during break times to assist students' skill development and understanding of social rules.

Break times can provide students with opportunities to socialize and engage in activities with their peers in a safe, supportive environment. When school members consistently model, encourage, and recognize appropriate social behaviors, they increase the likelihood of promoting positive behaviors and preventing bullying behaviors.

Schools can allow students to develop pro-social skills, extend key understandings about social rules, and practice behaving appropriately in both structured and semi-structured environments when they provide:

- A range of semi-structured indoor and outdoor activities
- Supervised activities for rainy days
- Recreational and hobby clubs
- Blogs managed by school staff

Ways schools can create more pro-social schoolyards include:

- Providing equipment that allows for different levels of challenging play
- Using attractive, age-appropriate outdoor equipment
- Facilitating greater use by students of available equipment

Step 1: Activity Review

Using Protective Physical Environment toolkit 6.3, list all the equipment (such as playground and sporting equipment) and activities (such as lunchtime concerts, teacher-led activities, and library access) that are available to students. Compile this list over several days involving as many staff as possible to ensure all activities and equipment available to students are captured.

For all equipment and activities, complete the "Who accesses?," "How could access be improved?," and "Comments" columns. Consider the following:

- What equipment and activities cater to developmental needs of students of all ages?
- How can this access be improved?
- Is there equity in the access to equipment and activities for all ages? If not, how can this be improved?
- Do students know in which areas they can spend their break times?
- Are students using these areas?
- Which groups of students would like to spend time in areas they are currently not allowed?
- Can provisions be made to accommodate these groups?

Step 2: Planning

Distribute the completed Protective Physical Environment toolkit 6.3 to staff, students, and parents to seek their input into the activities and equipment that are made available to students during break times to validate the initial list.

Using this information, work through Protective Physical Environment toolkit 6.4 to prioritize areas for improvement (for example, provision of new line markings on court areas and improved access to existing equipment and activities). This toolkit will help staff identify the areas of concern, suggest strategies to overcome these problem areas, and assign staff and a timeline for completing the changes.

 Students are encouraged to help younger students join in activities during break times.

Some students need support to join in activities in the schoolyard during break times. Engaging young people as leaders to facilitate activities during break times has many advantages.

Step 1: Engaging Students as Leaders

Students are powerful leaders in a school context and are largely underused by schools. To engage, train, and support student leaders, consider:

1. Choosing students who make good leaders and are already working toward leadership roles within the school or in the broader community
2. Identifying teacher mentors to manage the leadership programs and support and facilitate the student leader activities—The teacher mentor needs to have a good relationship with the students and be willing to support new and innovative ideas. It is important for the leaders to take ownership in initiating and directing ideas and activities.

3. Providing student leaders with time and space to meet to discuss their plans for the break time student-led activities
4. Allocating resources where necessary to implement their lunchtime activities
5. Providing ongoing support from the teacher mentor to the student leaders to develop and implement their activities

Step 2: Facilitating Interaction Between Leaders and Younger Students

To make the best use of volunteer leaders in both primary and secondary settings, encourage them to consult with staff and students to determine in what ways younger students need support. In a primary setting, leaders may be needed to keep a game going or to remind groups of the importance of following rules and the negotiation of any new rules. In the secondary setting, this may involve students mentoring new students, particularly at times of transition.

By developing programs in the primary setting that train volunteer leaders to assist younger students with group games (for example, managing equipment and refereeing, teaching new games, and joining in games), schools can:

- Provide older students with the opportunity to develop their leadership skills
- Increase students' sense of social responsibility
- Allow students to learn new skills
- Form new friendship groups with strong positive role models

In the secondary setting, these programs will:

- Develop decision-making skills among volunteer leaders
- Provide positive role models for younger students
- Develop opportunities for volunteers to be more socially responsible
- Establish positive connections across age groups

Step 3: Review

Regularly review with the student leaders and the students they are working with to determine the use of, and student satisfaction with, the leadership program. The review could consider asking a sample of the younger students the following questions:

- Did you engage in lunchtime activities with student leaders?
- What did you like about these activities?
- What new skills did you learn?
- What could be improved or done differently?
- Would you like to see this program modified? If so, in what ways?
- What activities could be implemented next term?

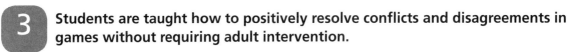 **Students are taught how to positively resolve conflicts and disagreements in games without requiring adult intervention.**

When conflict resolution skills are explicitly taught within classroom curriculum, some students experience increased levels of confidence and feel better supported to transfer these skills to the schoolyard. Conflict resolution is more successful when the people involved in the conflict are the ones involved in finding a solution. Schools that develop a simple, well-defined process that is understood and adhered to by all students are usually more successful when resolving conflicts. A powerful component of this process involves encouraging students to consider points of view other than their own and to endeavor to resolve conflict by ensuring everyone gets a fair go.

The following is an example of a conflict resolution process as used in the Friendly Schools and Supportive Schools curriculum resources (see Key Understandings and Competencies toolkit 5.1).

- Respect each other.
- Think about the problem.
- Listen to the other person.
- Say what you feel.
- Brainstorm solutions.
- Stick to what you have decided.
- Talk again if the solution is not working.

 4 **Supervised opportunities are provided for students to positively use technology for academic and social purposes.**

Cyberbullying is most likely to occur at home or during break times at school (Galen & Underwood, 1997) when young people are spending more time using technology for social purposes than academic purposes. While families need to be reminded of their responsibilities to support their children in cyberspace, young people and schools benefit from structured learning regarding the safer and effective use of technology for both academic and social purposes. As technology is constantly changing, the most effective learning is delivered in accordance with where they are spending time online. Teaching young people how to reduce their exposure to cyberbullying is important. School staff need to identify opportunities for young people to learn positive ways to use technology, especially to support someone who may have been cyberbullied. Many activities are provided in the Friendly Schools (primary) and Supportive Schools (secondary) classroom resources to increase student understandings and skills related to reducing harm from cyberbullying.

Opportunities to integrate teaching about positive technology use are included in the Friendly Schools and Supportive Schools curriculum resources, as described in Key Understandings and Competencies toolkit 5.1.

 5 **Outdoor areas, out-of-bounds areas, and "safer" areas are clearly identified to students, and students are encouraged to spend time in areas where adequate supervision is provided.**

Students and their families need to be informed of the reasons behind some of the decisions regarding where students can and cannot spend break times. When there are consistent messages and clear understandings around the use of the schoolyard, students are more likely to understand and respect the boundaries.

Using Protective Physical Environment toolkit 6.1, as described earlier, provides a clear representation of which areas are available to students.

Health and other student support services are located in areas that encourage student access.

Some students feel uncomfortable accessing health and support services due to the stigma that can sometimes be associated with service use. There is the potential for this to be more pronounced in secondary settings given young people's increased vulnerability to being teased or ridiculed for seeking help. Several factors can be considered to maximize students' willingness to access health and support services:

- Locate these services with other facilities commonly used by students (such as those located near teachers with a leadership role).
- Ensure service staff are trained to be approachable and skilled to help.
- Actively promote the proactive nature of the school's support services so that students are encouraged to use them at all times, not just when they are feeling vulnerable.
- Reassure students about the confidentiality of their visit.
- Design the service environment to be comfortable and welcoming to young people.

 Competent supervision is provided by school staff.

Encouraging students to spend time in areas where the level of adult supervision is high will reduce the invisibility of bullying behavior. Schoolwide data collection on the prevalence of bullying, including where and when bullying occurs, can be used to inform the provision of well-organized supervision from trained staff to ensure:

- Signs and symptoms of bullying are identified
- Situations are responded to in a timely manner
- Students feel safe
- All areas of the school grounds that students may access are visible to duty staff
- Hot spots are identified
- Out-of-bounds areas are defined
- Improved use of the schoolyard by all students

Building Capacity toolkit 2.1 describes surveys that could be used to identify where and when bullying occurs.

Questions to review staff supervision during break times:

- **Is there a formal reporting process or system for bullying incidents in the schoolyard?**
  Establish if one exists and define the benefits for your school of having a formal reporting system. See chapter 4 of *Evidence for Practice*, "Proactive Policies and Practices," for further information relating to the development of a reporting system.
- **To what extent are all staff, students, and parents aware of this reporting procedure?**
  Whole-school community awareness of the process of reporting incidents ensures effective and supported implementation across the school.
- **Is there a central register of all reported incidents in the schoolyard?**
  A central record system enables the effective recording, monitoring, and follow-up of bullying incidents.

- **Who maintains the record system, and what do they do with the information?**
  Assign the management of the central record system to a few key staff. The same key staff would ideally be trained in using the Shared Concern method and other restorative techniques to effectively respond to bullying incidents (see Proactive Policies and Practices toolkits 4.1, 4.2, and 4.3).

- **Is there a system to monitor reported incidents for emerging bullying behavior trends and repeat offenders?**
  Maintaining a central record system makes it easier for key staff to identify students who are repeatedly bullying others and those being bullied frequently as well as the locations where bullying is occurring. Monitoring reported incidents will also allow the school to identify bullying hot spots and modify schoolyard supervision accordingly.

Competent supervision across the school grounds is one of the most effective strategies to reduce bullying behavior. The following questions may help the school assess and refine its supervision strategies to help reduce and effectively manage bullying that occurs outside of the classroom.

- **Is there a coordinated and regularly updated supervision roster?**
  It is important that the on-duty staff and supervision roster is considered to be as important as staffing classrooms with appropriately trained staff. Supervision during break times must be consistent, supported by staff who are trained and know how to respond according to the school's behavior policies.

- **Are all staff trained to identify and respond effectively to bullying behavior?**
  Training staff in the school's preferred methods for reducing bullying incidents (from the behavior policies) before they conduct supervision duties at break times is important.

- **Are all staff trained in the school's system of recording incidents of bullying?**
  The whole-school community needs to be aware of the process of reporting incidents to ensure effective and supported implementation across the school.

- **Does the school use bright duty teacher vests to help students quickly and easily identify support staff?**
  Schools have found that having duty teachers clearly visible to other staff and students makes students feel safer. Students report it is also easier to identify a teacher when they need one.

8   **Targeted professional learning is provided for duty teachers to identify and respond appropriately and effectively to bullying situations.**

Duty teachers are often the first on the scene at a bullying incident and, therefore, need to know how to respond in a way consistent with the school's behavioral policies. As supervisors can include nonteaching staff and relief teachers, induction processes and professional learning opportunities need to be offered to all staff. This training should address the school's behavioral policies and response including:

- Identification of bullying incidents
- Ways to communicate with students to gain a better understanding of what has happened and who is involved
- Immediate responses to ensure the safety of all students
- Strategies to acknowledge positive bystander responses
- Methods of reporting that are consistent with the school policy
- Referral pathways and effective referral strategies
- Strategies for student support and follow-up

Chapter 7

Strengthening Family Links

Involving students and families in the school's strategies to address bullying will increase the chance of achieving lasting behavior change in students. Some ways to achieve this include:

- Involving students' families in the school's operations where practical and appropriate
- Creating opportunities for input into school planning and policy
- Planning activities to ensure regular positive communication
- Using numerous channels of communication to reach all families
- Cooperating closely with families to ensure early recognition of the signs and symptoms of bullying and determining those students who may be at increased risk of involvement in bullying
- Collaborating with families to resolve specific instances of bullying and provide targeted support to the student involved in bullying and his or her family
- Acknowledging differences in family, parent, and community priorities

Strategies for Good Practice: Strengthening Family Links

1. Schools provide regular, positive communication to engage families and encourage their involvement.
2. Students invite families to school events and activities.
3. The school's response to reducing bullying is developed in collaboration with families.
4. There is close cooperation between the school and families in responding to specific bullying situations that arise.
5. Families and the community are encouraged to consistently demonstrate an intolerance of bullying behavior.

 Schools provide regular, positive communication to engage families and encourage their involvement.

Establishing and maintaining open channels of regular, positive communication with families leads to the development of a school culture that values their important contribution. Leaders that recognize diverse cultures in their school community will make use of multiple communication channels, including the translation of written materials to reach the whole-school community. This is particularly important prior to and following student transition from primary to secondary school. Families are also becoming more open to using electronic communication via email or school portals where regular information and active links to resources can be provided to families.

Regular communication with families:

- Ensures they are continually updated with current information on policy development and organization
- Encourages conversations across school and home
- Fosters curiosity for schools and families to learn about each other
- Helps them feel valued and respected as real partners who can help solve problems
- Increases their willingness to become involved on a number of levels, bringing their many and varied skills into the school
- Builds positive relationships
- Makes parents feel welcome at school
- Cements common understandings related to school, family, and community priorities and actions to reduce bullying

Use the School–Family–Community Partnerships toolkit 7.1 to survey families to determine how welcome they feel at the school. Try to accommodate, where possible, families who do not speak English as a first language. Collate the results and appoint a committee comprised of parent, principal, and teacher representatives to decide how best to use the information. Formulate and implement recommendations to help parents feel more welcome in the school. This set of questions could be used in conjunction with whole-school assessment strategies described in Building Capacity toolkit 2.1.

Family communication sheets can provide the impetus for family discussion about school matters, including increasing communication and reducing bullying. School–Family–Community Partnerships toolkits 7.2 and 7.3 include two family communication sheets that can be included in the school's newsletter, which can be enlarged to create posters displayed in areas of the school used by families, or distributed to families in need of support regarding communication strategies and bullying behavior. In addition, Supportive School Culture toolkits 3.1 and 3.2 provide further examples of ways to communicate with parents through newsletter and assembly items.

 Students invite families to school events and activities.

Many parents comment that the only time they are invited to the school, especially in secondary schools, is when their child is behaving inappropriately or there is some other problem. It can be valuable to ask families how they want to be involved with the school, find out which days and times suit them better, and ask how they would like to receive communications.

Inviting families to special activities, in addition to assemblies, that provide positive experiences, will help them feel more comfortable and welcome in the school and more inclined to make return visits. This is particularly beneficial following the transition to secondary school when students may feel disconnected to their new school. Invite families to events using the natural groupings that occur within the school, for example, send invitations to a meet-and-greet through student pastoral care/ tutor groups, so families feel they have a group to which they can belong, especially if the tutor group remains together for a number of years. Attendance by parents is always better when their children are performing, when children personally invite their parents via a letter or something similar, and when child care is provided.

Some activities used effectively by schools include:

- Family sports days
- Special assemblies (for example, grandparents' day)
- ICT information or social media workshops with students and families (these work well when students are involved in or lead the presentations)
- Expert guest speaker presentations discussing topics with families such as cyberbullying and cyber safety

When families feel strong connections to schools, they are more confident and willing to work in partnership with schools to support their children's learning. In addition to traditional school-home communication opportunities, the Friendly Schools and Families project distributed family communication and activity sheets that focused on family and school connectedness, parent-child engagement, and communication pointers. The aim of these sheets was to increase the level and quality of communication between parents and their children, such that parents were more receptive to school communication and thus were more informed of and attended more school events.

One way to engage families in the development of a supportive school culture is to host a family friendship carnival, as described in School–Family–Community Partnerships toolkit 7.5. The aim of the carnival is to involve staff, students, and parents in activities designed to encourage all school community members to practice and enhance social skills in a fun and nonthreatening environment.

 ### 3 The school's response to reducing bullying is developed in collaboration with families.

Many parents are concerned about the effects of bullying on their children; however, they are often unsure how to help their children prevent bullying and respond effectively, especially when the bullying is perpetrated via technology, as with cyberbullying. By involving parents in the development of behavior policies (see Proactive Policies and Practices toolkit 4.5) that relate to bullying (and other issues) schools can strengthen the likely impact of these policies on student behavior. By working together, the whole-school community can:

- Foster positive attitudes and friendlier schools
- Develop a safe and happy environment for students
- Encourage students and adults to talk about bullying
- Let students know that bullying is unacceptable behavior anywhere in the community

Schools can create links with families and communities by providing targeted information sessions that educate families about how to:

- Work in collaboration with schools to develop students' social skills
- Help their children initiate and maintain positive friendships, both online and offline
- Respond effectively if their child is being bullied either online or offline
- Respond effectively if their child is bullying others (including siblings)
- Use social media in positive ways

These strategies demonstrate to parents the strong commitment of school leaders to establishing a positive school culture where all members feel safe, valued, and supported. It is important for students to see their parents and the school working together with a common desire to help them feel safer, happier, and supported at school. This partnership will be most effective when parents:

- Encourage children to talk about online and offline bullying, both at school and at home
- Cooperate with class teachers to share valuable information about how their children are feeling
- Talk and work with their children's school to help achieve the most positive outcome for their children
- Become familiar with their school's bullying and cyberbullying policy, which should outline how the school plans to respond to these behaviors

In Supportive School Culture toolkit 3.4, the role of bystanders is discussed and could be shared with parents to help them understand how their children can help reduce bullying behavior. In addition, Supportive School Culture toolkit 3.5 provides information about the development of assertiveness skills in students to increase self-esteem and confidence.

There is close cooperation between the school and families in responding to specific bullying situations that arise.

When schools and families cooperate in responding to specific bullying incidents, a positive outcome is more likely. This demonstrates the school's commitment to resolving the problem collaboratively, in a transparent and consistent manner. Chapter 4 of *Evidence for Practice*, which includes Proactive Policies and Practices toolkit 4.5, and chapter 7 of *Evidence for Practice* describe ways that parents and caregivers of the bullying target or targets, the perpetrators, and the bystanders can be effectively involved in the school's response to a bullying incident, especially if the incident is severe.

Parents can:

- Discuss with their children positive ways to develop and maintain friendships
- Encourage children to think about how bullying behavior makes others feel
- Explain the concepts of respect, cooperation, and negotiation

Parents can be encouraged to use the following questions when specific bullying situations arise:

- If you saw your friend being teased, how would you feel? What could you do?
- If your friend asked you to help bully another child, how would this make you feel? What could you do?
- Who would you talk to if you were bullied?
- What would you do if you were bullied?

When a bullying situation arises, it is important to separate the child and the behavior and that students are not labeled as bullies. By doing so, the message students receive is that bullying is a bad behavior, not that a student who bullies is a bad person. It is easy to focus on "busting" the bullies; however, a strategy like the Shared Concern method, which promotes and demonstrates how to solve problems and find positive solutions, is usually more effective and likely to lead to longer-term positive behavior change.

Restorative techniques such as the Support Group method and Shared Concern method are beneficial if parents understand their purpose and expected outcomes. School–Family–Community Partnerships toolkit 7.4 describes the Shared Concern method in a format suitable for families and school staff and contains an additional family activity that may assist in reinforcing the process followed in this technique to resolve relationship conflicts. Proactive Policies and Practices toolkits 4.1 and 4.2 provide information about these techniques in more detail for school staff.

Section 1

When children are bullied, parents can assist their children and the school by supporting the identification of a group of people (support group) their child feels comfortable talking with and turning to for help. Role-playing what they would say if they approached these people about a bullying situation will help students feel more comfortable seeking support and reassure parents their children have the skills to ask for help if they need it. This group generally includes:

- Parents
- Classroom teacher
- Teachers on duty at recess or lunchtime
- Other school staff members
- School friends
- Family friends

CHPRC research found that it was valuable for the school to always advise parents if a bullying incident occurred that involved their children, similar to the process a school would use if a student was to visit the school health center for an illness or injury during the day. Depending on the severity of the incident it may not be necessary for the parents to visit the school, but they should at least be apprised of the school's action in response to the incident. This communication allows parents to be well aware of incidents and the actions by the school, and also helps parents talk with their children following these incidents.

 5 Families and the community are encouraged to consistently demonstrate an intolerance of bullying behavior.

To change behavior, bullying reduction strategies need to focus not only on the school environment but also include the home and community. Parents can:

- Encourage children to talk about bullying both at school and at home
- Cooperate with class teachers to share valuable information about how their children are feeling
- Talk and work with the school to help achieve the most positive outcome for their child
- Become familiar with the school's bullying policy

Building a consistent, positive community response that actively discourages bullying behavior may require a shift in attitudes and knowledge about the harms associated with this behavior for both the target and the perpetrator. To achieve this normative change, teachers, families, and the wider community need to be aware of what behaviors constitute bullying, especially covert bullying such as social exclusion, rumor spreading, and cyberbullying. They also need to know what action to take if they see a bullying incident and to be aware of what young people perceive if adults take no action when bullying occurs. If an adult observes bullying behavior or other forms of aggression and takes no action, there is a likelihood this behavior will continue and may intensify compared to a situation where there is no adult present. This has important implications for the whole-school community, which may be seen by students to be condoning bullying through their inaction when the behavior occurs in their presence.

The whole-school community can send a strong, consistent message about bullying, when stakeholders are provided with:

- Current evidence-based information about bullying behavior
- Open and encouraging invitations to attend meetings to discuss bullying behavior and engage in decision making regarding possible school actions
- Ongoing information about school action, progress, and policy

Chapter 8

Developing Social and Emotional Learning in the Classroom

CYBER—BULLYING BECAME
A NATIONAL CRISIS WHEN
SOCIAL NETWORKING SITES
INTRODUCED THE "HATE" BUTTON

The overview on the following pages is organized into the five key areas of the social and emotional learning model, for students aged four to six. Each key area differentiates the age-appropriate focus for students aged either four to five or five to six and what each focus will enable students to do.

Each focus is developed into a teaching and learning sequence in sections 2 and 3 of this teacher resource book.

Teachers are encouraged to decide on an appropriate starting point based on their students' current social and emotional learning skills and understandings.

Overview of the Five Key Areas for Social and Emotional Learning for Middle Childhood Ages 8–10		
Key Area 1: Self-Awareness Sense of Self, Emotional Awareness		
Age	**Focus**	**This Focus Will Enable Students to:**
Ages 8–9 **Section 2** **page 60**	1. My self-esteem	• Define self-esteem • List factors that can contribute to positive self-esteem • Demonstrate actions they can take to help themselves feel better • Demonstrate how helping others can also be good for their self-esteem
	2. Physical and emotional health	• Describe the difference between physical and emotional health • Classify hurtful situations according to whether they cause harm physically, emotionally, or both • Demonstrate ways they and others can minimize physical or emotional hurt
	3. When my feelings are hurt	• Describe situations that may hurt their feelings • Identify positive actions they can take when their feelings are hurt • Demonstrate ways to help themselves feel better
	4. Safe or unsafe feelings	• Identify feelings that help them recognize when they are safe • Identify feelings that warn them they are not in a safe situation • Describe when and where they feel safe and unsafe at school • Demonstrate when they need to ask an adult for help • Use strategies to keep themselves safe in social situations
Ages 9–10 **Section 3** **page 126**	1. Exploring my values	• Identify values that are meaningful to them • Describe the importance of applying their values beyond the classroom to the wider community • Demonstrate putting their values into practice in social situations
	2. Values and manners online and offline	• Identify manners and the role manners play in their lives • Describe common manners expected by the society in which they live • Demonstrate appropriate manners in all situations
	3. Values and social rules	• Identify social rules • Explain the reasons these rules exist • Demonstrate how to use social rules in different situations
	4. Values in my community	• Identify values relating to being part of their community • Describe the characteristics of a community whose members value each other's differences • Demonstrate ways they can help others in their community

Key Area 2: Self-Management Emotional Regulation, Resilience, and Self-Motivation		
Age	**Focus**	**This Focus Will Enable Students to:**
Ages 8–9 **Section 2** **page 78**	1. Managing our feelings	• Explain why it is important to learn to manage their feelings • Describe the positive and negative ways in which their bodies can react to feelings • Demonstrate ways of managing their feelings
	2. Positive thinking	• Identify factors that can spoil a good day • Demonstrate positive actions they can take to turn a not-so-good day into a better day • Identify self-talk that can make them feel better about themselves
	3. Perseverance	• Define perseverance • Describe situations where perseverance is needed • Demonstrate an ability to persevere in challenging situations
Ages 9–10 **Section 3** **page 146**	1. Resolving conflict	• Identify positive actions they can take to resolve conflicts • Describe the difference between win-win, win-lose, and lose-lose conflict resolution • Demonstrate strategies to use in win-win conflict resolution
	2. When it's OK to say "no"	• Identify the types of situations when it's OK to say "no" • Predict the effect on themselves and others of saying "no" in social situations • Demonstrate saying "no" confidently in role-play situations
	3. Standing up for what you believe in and value	• Identify situations that challenge what they believe in and value • Describe how the decisions they make can be influenced by their values • Predict ways to maintain positive control of their emotions in challenging situations • Demonstrate positive responses that reflect their personal values in response to conflict situations

Key Area 3: Social Awareness Understanding and Interpreting Social Situations		
Age	**Focus**	**This Focus Will Enable Students to:**
Ages 8–9 **Section 2** **page 92**	1. Giving—Making deposits	• Identify the value of giving to and sharing with others • Describe how their friendly behaviors—taking turns, sharing, speaking in a friendly way, listening to others' ideas, and caring about others and their feelings—can lead to positive feelings for themselves • Demonstrate ways to develop and maintain positive friendship groups using their friendly behaviors
	2. Making things better	• Identify times when they or others are not being treated nicely • Describe what someone can do to feel better when being treated unkindly • Demonstrate ways to feel better when treated unkindly
Ages 9–10 **Section 3** **page 160**	1. Friends and friendship groups	• Identify reciprocal friends and friendship groups • Describe the influence of values on friendship and positive friendship groups • Demonstrate actions they can take to promote positive communication and cooperation in friendship groups
	2. Equality and exclusion in groups	• Identify fairness, equality, and exclusion in groups • Describe behaviors and attitudes that reflect treating people fairly and equally • Demonstrate fostering a culture of fairness and equality within our school community
	3. Empathy—Understanding how others feel	• Identify times when they need to try to understand how others may be feeling • Predict how others may be feeling • Apply strategies to demonstrate their understanding of others' feelings

Key Area 4: Relationship Skills Positive Relationship Skills		
Age	**Focus**	**This Focus Will Enable Students to:**
Ages 8–9 **Section 2** **page 100**	1. Bullying behaviors	• Describe the characteristics of specific types of bullying behavior • Predict whether a behavior is bullying or not bullying • Demonstrate the ability to distinguish between and respond to bullying and nonbullying behaviors
	2. Bullying—Keeping safe	• Identify if a behavior is bullying or not bullying • Describe ways to assess potential risks before responding to a bullying situation • Demonstrate safe actions to take as a bystander to a bullying situation
	3. How does it feel to be bullied?	• Identify feelings others may experience as a result of being bullied • Describe the possible physical and mental effects of bullying behavior • Demonstrate actions they can take to discourage bullying behavior
Ages 9–10 **Section 3** **page 176**	1. Behaviors that are bullying	• Identify bullying behaviors • Describe the characteristics of bullying behavior • Demonstrate actions they can take and who they can go to for help in a bullying situation
	2. Who is involved in bullying?	• Identify who is involved in bullying situations • Describe the roles of the key players involved in a bullying situation • Demonstrate safe actions key players can take to reduce bullying
	3. Why some people bully but most people don't	• Identify reasons some people bully but most people don't • Describe how they feel about bullying behavior • Demonstrate positive alternatives to inappropriate, antisocial, and bullying behavior
	4. Bystanders to bullying	• Identify the decisions a bystander can make when he or she sees bullying, including cyberbullying • Describe the role of the bystander and the influence he or she can have on bullying situations • Demonstrate safe, positive bystander actions in bullying situations

Key Area 5: Social Decision Making Social Information Processing		
Age	**Focus**	**This Focus Will Enable Students to:**
Ages 8–9 **Section 2** **page 114**	1. Choices and consequences	• Demonstrate the use of a choices and consequences model to select appropriate actions to take to respond to bullying situations
	2. Responding safely to bullying situations	• Identify when it is safe to respond to a bullying situation • Describe strategies they can use to respond in a safe way to a bullying situation • Plan strategies to effectively respond to bullying situations • Demonstrate actions to take to reduce harm caused by bullying
Ages 9–10 **Section 3** **page 198**	1. Taking steps to help solve social problems	• Identify times when they can safely take action to discourage bullying as a bystander to a bullying situation • Describe the steps involved in the decision-making model • Demonstrate, using the decision-making model, that they can decide how to deal with bullying behavior

Organization of the Teaching and Learning Resources

The following two sections of teaching and learning resources are organized as follows.

Section 2 has the teaching and learning resources designed to develop the social and emotional learning skills for students ages eight to nine.

Section 3 has the teaching and learning resources which build on the social and emotional learning skills of students ages nine to ten.

The sections are divided into the five key areas, which are each developed into a sequence of learning focus.

- Key area 1: Self-awareness
- Key area 2: Self-management
- Key area 3: Social awareness
- Key area 4: Relationship skills
- Key area 5: Social decision making

It is recommended that teachers teach from each of the social and emotional learning key areas in the order presented, as understanding and skills in one key area are required to enable learning in another. An example of this is when students are developing social decision-making skills, they use their developed self-awareness, self-management, and social-awareness skills.

Following the cartoon, which illustrates a concept for the key area, is a brief description of the overall understandings and skills for this social and emotional learning area.

A table in the beginning of each key area briefly describes the emphasis of each learning focus and the outcomes the proposed focus activities will enable students to achieve.

The title of each focus summarizes the key messages and elaborates on what the focus will enable students to do.

A comprehensive list of focus activities follows a learning sequence of introducing, developing, and reflecting on the key messages and recommends the resources needed, including suggested sample texts and activity and resource sheets (online at **go.solution-tree.com/behavior** and in appendices A and B).

Teachers are encouraged to teach from each of the social and emotional learning focus areas in the order presented, as each builds on the vocabulary, concepts, and skills covered in preceding focus areas.

The learning sequence for each focus includes:

- **Introducing key messages**—Sets the context for the activity and introduces the key messages to help students link previous social and emotional learning to new knowledge and skills. Icons indicate the type of activity such as literature.
- **Developing key messages**—Provides students with opportunities to develop and practice key messages, relevant social and emotional understandings, and skills. Visit **go.solution-tree.com /behavior** for reproducibles of the student activity sheets linked to these learning activities.
- **Reflecting on key messages**—Encourages students to reflect and record their thoughts, feelings, and attitudes throughout the course of their social and emotional learning in a student journal. Teachers are also encouraged to reflect on the extent to which students have understood the key messages for each focus.

Visit **go.solution-tree.com/behavior** for student reproducibles of the activity sheets and teacher resource sheets.

Using the Resource

Research clearly shows that the greater the dose of social and emotional learning, the better the outcomes for students. As such, the greater the number of learning activities completed in each focus area, the greater the likelihood students can achieve the social and emotional learning outcomes.

Teachers are encouraged to determine the social and emotional learning needs of their students to ensure the activities chosen meet students' developmental levels, understandings, and competencies. While it is recommended to teach the key areas in the sequence they are presented, it may also be important to consider the school's vision, priorities, and values in deciding which activities to teach as well as local curriculum requirements.

With this knowledge, teachers can review the activities provided within the resource to decide which activities in each focus area they can implement, select alternative resources, integrate into an appropriate learning area, and gather evidence of students' developing understandings and skills to inform future practice.

Teaching and Learning Resources

Middle Childhood

Teacher Resource
Ages 8–9

Self-Awareness

Sense of Self, Emotional Awareness

Self-awareness skills help us to recognize and understand our feelings while valuing our strengths and abilities. This involves:

- Being able to identify what we are feeling
- Understanding why we might feel a certain way
- Recognizing and having confidence to use our strengths and abilities

Key Area 1: Self-Awareness

Focus	This Focus Will Enable Students to:	Focus Activities
1. My self-esteem	• Define self-esteem • List factors that can contribute to positive self-esteem • Demonstrate actions they can take to help themselves feel better • Demonstrate how helping others can also be good for their self-esteem	• Literature and discussion • Banking your self-esteem • Papier-mâché piggy bank • Journal
2. Physical and emotional health	• Describe the difference between physical and emotional health • Classify hurtful situations according to whether they cause harm physically, emotionally, or both • Demonstrate ways they and others can minimize physical or emotional hurt	• Explosion chart—Staying healthy • Picture study • Healthy body, healthy mind • Game—Ouch! That Hurts! • Journal
3. When my feelings are hurt	• Describe situations that may hurt their feelings • Identify positive actions they can take when their feelings are hurt • Demonstrate ways to help themselves feel better	• Feel good, positive talk bandages • Poster • Journal
4. Safe or unsafe feelings	• Identify feelings that help them recognize when they are safe • Identify feelings that warn them they are not in a safe situation • Describe when and where they feel safe and unsafe at school • Demonstrate when they need to ask an adult for help • Use strategies to keep themselves safe in social situations	• Literature and discussion • Mapping our thoughts • Mapping safe actions at school • Journal

Key Area 1: Self-Awareness

Sense of Self, Emotional Awareness

Focus 1: My Self-Esteem

Key Messages

How we feel about ourselves is called *self-esteem*.

By the way we think, the way we feel, and the way we act, we can affect our self-esteem.

This focus will enable students to:

- Define self-esteem
- List factors that can contribute to positive self-esteem
- Demonstrate actions they can take to help themselves feel better
- Demonstrate how helping others can also be good for their self-esteem

Focus 1 Activities	Resources Needed
Introducing Key Messages	
Literature	Resource sheet: "Story of Young Wilbur Chapman and His Pig Pete" (Leprosy Mission Canada, n.d.)
Banking your self-esteem	Paper, writing materials
Developing Key Messages	
Papier-mâché piggy bank	See activity for materials.
Reflecting on Key Messages	
Journal	Journal, writing materials

Introducing Key Messages

Explain to the students that the first piggy banks were not just about saving money; they were about caring for and helping other people. Explain how the story about young Wilbur and his pig will show how the piggy bank was a symbol of saving to help others and has continued as a symbol for us to save for our future.

Literature

Story of Young Wilbur Chapman and His Pig Pete (Leprosy Mission Canada, n.d.)

Read the story of young Wilbur Chapman and his pig Pete to students. (See the "Story of Young Wilbur Chapman and His Pig Pete" resource sheet.)

After Reading

Explain to students that the way we feel about ourselves is called our self-esteem. We can increase (deposit) or decrease (withdrawal) our self-esteem by the way we think, the way we feel, and the way we act, just like a personal piggy bank. For example, being congratulated after doing something brave, like a public speech, can make you feel good about yourself. This is a deposit to your self-esteem. Some situations and experiences can make you feel sad or bad about yourself, such as being excluded from friendship groups. This can be a withdrawal from your self-esteem and is like having someone take money from your piggy bank. You can also make a deposit into someone else's self-esteem with friendly behavior like sharing and including others in your games.

Activity—Banking Your Self-Esteem

Arrange the students into pairs and give each pair two sheets of paper on which students write the headings _Deposits_ and _Withdrawals_. Students then discuss and record (on the appropriate sheet) actions by themselves and others they would classify as either a deposit or a withdrawal to their own or someone else's self-esteem. Display students' deposit sheets around the room to remind students throughout the year of positive actions they can take to make deposits to their own and others' self-esteem.

- **Example Deposits:** Being complimented on your artwork, asked to join the choir, invited to a special party, and congratulating yourself on a job well done
- **Example Withdrawals:** Thinking you are not good at anything, having your feelings hurt by someone calling you nasty names, deliberately being left out of a group, and your friends telling untrue stories about you

Developing Key Messages

Activity—Papier-Mâché Piggy Bank

More than one day will be needed to complete this activity to allow time for drying. Assistance from parent volunteers or older students is also recommended.

Materials

- Balloons (one per student)
- Old newspapers
- A paper egg carton (one carton per two students)
- Masking tape
- Flour-water glue (made according to the following instructions)
- Pink paint and brushes
- Pink pipe cleaners (one per student)
- A craft knife
- Plastic googly eyes or buttons
- Pens

Instructions

1. **Flour-water glue**: Mix one cup of flour with one cup of water. When this mixture is thin and runny, stir it into four cups of boiling water. Leave to cool after simmering for a few minutes.

2. **Newspaper**: Help students tear the old newspapers into strips of about one inch width (length is not important).

3. **Balloon body**: Blow up a balloon for each student, but avoid blowing it up too much. Using the flour-water glue, students glue the strips of newspaper so that the balloon is completely covered with a few layers. Leave to dry, and then use a pin to pop the balloon.

4. **Legs and snout**: Add legs and a snout to the piggy bank by separating five sections of the paper egg carton, and attaching them to the body with masking tape.

5. **Paint**: Students can paint the piggy bank with pink paint (or could glue on pink tissue paper). Leave to dry.

6. **Tail**: Teacher or parents make a small hole in the tail end of the pig. Students can insert pipe cleaners into the hole and shape them to look like a spiral.

7. **Eyes**: Eyes can be added using plastic googly eyes, buttons, paint, or a black pen.

8. **Nostrils**: Students can draw two nostrils on the snout of the pig.

9. **Money slot**: Teacher or parents cut a slot in the top of the pig's body. This should be large enough for students to push through pieces of paper.

Section 2

Students deposit ideas from the brainstorm sheets developed earlier and new ideas generated throughout the year. Students can retrieve positive ideas to build their self-esteem in their piggy bank by shaking out the ideas when they and their friends need them, or a hole and plug could be added to the underside of the piggy bank. Students could also decide to make a class piggy bank and decide on a project or charity they will contribute to throughout the year.

Reflecting on Key Messages

Student Journal

Introduce students to the journal they will use to complete activities throughout the year.

Students draw a piggy bank and record examples of deposits they have received during the day or week.

Teacher Reflection

How effectively were the key messages developed?

To what extent are your students now able to:

- Define self-esteem?
- List factors that can contribute to positive self-esteem?
- Demonstrate actions they can take to help themselves feel better?
- Demonstrate how helping others can also be good for their self-esteem?

Focus 2: Physical and Emotional Health

Key Messages

You can be hurt physically or feel hurt emotionally (in your body or your mind), but there are actions you can take to help manage and reduce this hurt.

This focus will enable students to:

- Describe the difference between physical and emotional health
- Classify hurtful situations according to whether they cause harm physically, emotionally, or both
- Demonstrate ways they and others can minimize physical or emotional hurt

Focus 3 Activities	Resources Needed
Introducing Key Messages	
Explosion chart—Staying healthy	
Developing Key Messages	
Picture study	Old magazines, scissors, glue, paper, or personal journals
Healthy body, healthy mind	Paper, writing materials
Game—Ouch! That Hurts!	Resource sheet: "Ouch! That Hurts!" Resource sheet: "'I Could Try . . .' Cards"
Reflecting on Key Messages	
Journal	Journal, writing materials

Section 2

Introducing Key Messages

Explain to students that to understand more about how we can make deposits to our self-esteem, we need to understand a little more about physical and emotional health.

Being physically healthy means:

- Your body feels good
- Your body parts work well

Being emotionally healthy means:

- Feeling good about yourself
- Feeling loved and cared for
- Feeling like you belong in a group

Activity

Discuss with the students how people experience different feelings. When people are hurt physically they feel pain in their body, such as in their arm or their leg. When they are hurt emotionally, their feelings are hurt; they might say, "I feel sad when my baby brother is sick" or "I feel upset about losing my favorite book."

Stress the importance of taking the time to think about how our actions may affect others physically and emotionally.

Use the following example:

Jackie, a new girl, has come to school wearing a different uniform. You think she looks a bit silly in her old school uniform and think of something funny that you could say to make the class laugh. But then you think, "How would I feel if I had just started at this school and didn't have the correct uniform yet?" and instead you say to Jackie, "Hey, I like the colors of your uniform."

Activity—Explosion Chart: Staying Healthy

Ask the students to think about what we need to do to keep our bodies feeling good and our body parts working well (to keep physically healthy). Write the students' responses on a chart.

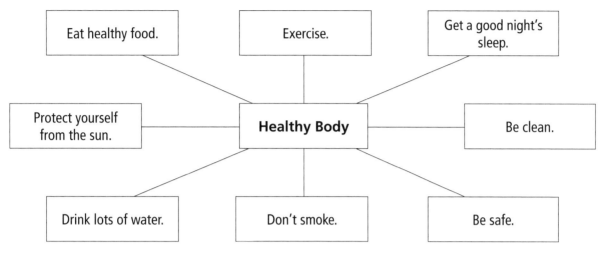

Figure 2: Healthy body chart.

Ask the students to think about how we look after our feelings (emotional health). Write their responses on a chart.

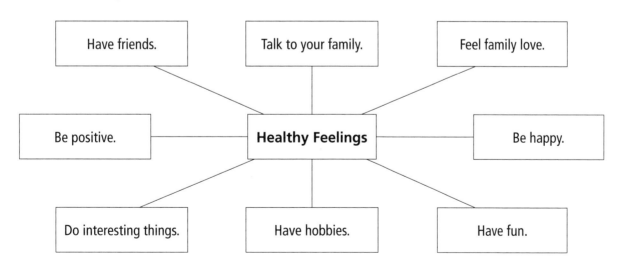

Figure 3: Healthy feelings chart.

Section 2

Developing Key Messages

Activity—Picture Study

Give the students some old magazines and a sheet of paper each (or use a page in their personal journal). Write the headings *Our Body* and *Our Mind* and ask the students to find and cut out different pictures representing their body (physical health) and their mind (emotional health), such as people eating a healthy meal, smiling, having fun with friends, and being loving.

Students classify and glue the pictures under the appropriate heading. Invite students to share their finished work and explain why they chose those images to represent the different health areas.

Activity—Healthy Body, Healthy Mind

Arrange the students into small groups. Give each group two small pieces of paper. Have someone in the group write the words *Hurt Body* on one piece of paper and another student write *Hurt Feelings* on the other. Read the following situations aloud, and allow time to discuss if the situation would hurt a person physically, emotionally, or both. After students have discussed the question with their group ask the students to take turns to hold up the sign for either *Hurt Body* or *Hurt Feelings* when you ask the question, "How was _____ hurting? Physically or emotionally?"

Stress that students also have the option of holding up both cards together.

Use the following example:

a) Aaron was riding his bike. He bumped into John and knocked him over. John had a cut on his arm, and it hurt.
    How was Aaron hurting? Physically or emotionally?
    Why?

b) Taylor felt hurt when one of her friends did not invite her to her birthday party.
    How was Taylor hurting? Physically or emotionally?
    Why?

c) Jack felt hurt when some students in the class laughed when he gave the wrong answer.
    How was Jack hurting? Physically or emotionally?
    Why?

d) Suki's dog bit her on the leg, and it hurt.
    How was Suki hurting? Physically or emotionally?
    Why?

e) Jaslyn was hurt when some students called her a nasty name.
    How was Jaslyn hurting? Physically or emotionally?
    Why?

f) Radjid fell over at basketball and grazed his knee. It hurt. Then, some kids on the team laughed, and that hurt too.
    How was Radjid hurting? Physically or emotionally?
    Why?

Discuss with students that when we injure ourselves, pain is our body's way of telling us something is wrong. When our feelings are hurt, we can feel distress in our mind if we tell ourselves negative things. For example, if someone says something mean to us, we might say to ourselves, "That person doesn't like me, and that makes me feel sad. My feelings are hurt."

Using the following situation as an example, ask the students to think about situations that can hurt their feelings and think about why they might feel hurt but also how else they can think about the situation to minimize any hurt.

- **Taylor felt hurt when one of her friends did not invite her to her birthday party.**
  Taylor may have told herself that her classmate did not like her anymore because she did not invite her to the party. This thought may have caused Taylor to feel upset and sad. Ask students to think about other less hurtful reasons why Taylor might not have been invited, for example, her classmate was only allowed to invite a small number of friends so she couldn't invite everyone from the class.

  Ask the students to think about what each of the children in the following situations may have thought that may have hurt their feelings. Have students think of other less hurtful ways to think about why this incident may have happened.

- **Jack felt hurt when some students in the class laughed when he gave the wrong answer.**
  Another way that Jack could think about this that would help him feel better: "That was a pretty funny answer now that I think about it." Jack laughs along too.

- **Jaslyn was hurt when some students called her a nasty name.**
  Another way that Jaslyn could think about this that would help her feel better: "That is not a very nice name. I don't like it, but I am not going to let it worry me."

Section 2

- **Radjid fell over at basketball and grazed his knee. It hurt. Then, some kids on the team laughed, and that hurt too.**
  Another way that Radjid could think about this that would help him feel better: "Wow, that hurt my knee, and that is not funny, but I must have looked pretty funny flying through the air."

Activity—Game: Ouch! That Hurts!

Arrange the class into pairs. Each pair receives one copy of a precut and laminated double-sided "Ouch! That Hurts!" resource sheet. The purpose of this game is to help students distinguish between emotional and physical pain and to match actions that could be taken to lessen the type of pain identified. One student in each pair reads a short scenario to his or her partner. Include two blank cards per pair, and encourage students to write short scenarios to be used when this game is played again. One partner then decides if the scenario represents physical or emotional pain. The ticked box on the reverse side of the situation cards is the correct answer and can be confirmed by the reader. After students have classified the type of hurt, they should try to match an action that could be taken to lessen the harm from the list of actions on the "'I Could Try . . .' Cards" resource sheet. It may be useful to cut and laminate these cards and prepare a set on a ring for each group.

Reflecting on Key Messages

Student Journal

Ask the students to illustrate and write three sentences about a time when they were hurt physically, emotionally, or both. For each example, students can write about how they could think more positively about the situation or what action they could take to lessen the hurt.

Teacher Reflection

How effectively were the key messages developed?

To what extent are your students now able to:

- Describe the difference between physical and emotional health?
- Classify hurtful situations according to whether they cause harm physically, emotionally, or both?
- Demonstrate ways they and others can minimize physical or emotional hurt?

Focus 3: When My Feelings Are Hurt

Key Messages

When my feelings are hurt, there are actions I can take to make myself feel better.

This focus will enable students to:

- Describe situations that may hurt their feelings
- Identify positive actions they can take when their feelings are hurt
- Demonstrate ways to help themselves feel better

Focus 3 Activities	Resources Needed
Introducing Key Messages	
Feel good, positive talk bandages	Bandages, pens, first aid kit
Developing Key Messages	
Poster	Paper, drawing and writing materials
Reflecting on Key Messages	
Journal	Journal, writing materials

Introducing Key Messages

Explain to the students that if we fall over and hurt ourselves, we sometimes need a first aid kit to help make us better. We might use bandages and some antiseptic cream to help make a scrape heal more quickly. Show your students one of the school's first aid kits.

Explain that when your feelings are hurt, and you are sad or upset, there are actions you can take to make yourself feel better. Ask the students to think about the following situations and what they could do to make themselves feel better.

- You are upset because you have no one to play with you.
- You are very sad because your dog is getting old and is very sick.
- You are being teased about the way your hair looks.

Discuss how using a bandage when you are hurt can make you feel better, not just for physical pain but also emotional pain. When you put on a bandage, people notice that something is wrong.

So a brighter bandage may have better healing power. When you are wearing a bright bandage on your sore knee, people will notice and ask, "Ooh, what happened to your knee?" Then you can tell them all about it and get some emotional care as well. Therefore, bandages can also be a symbol for emotional support.

Activity—Feel Good, Positive Talk Bandages

For this activity, you will give each student a bandage. Fluorescent bandages are the best bandages for this activity. Plain bandages are also suitable. Students will write in pen or permanent fine felt-tipped pen on these bandages.

Please be aware: Some students are allergic to bandages, so it is best to have them use a different material.

With examples, explain to students what a "feel good" statement sounds like. Everyone needs to hear positive words to feel good about him- or herself. When someone says to you, "I really like you as my friend," it makes you feel better about yourself. Talking nicely to yourself is called positive self-talk and counts as a deposit in your self-esteem piggy bank. It is important to practice talking positively to yourself throughout your life. If you put yourself down or talk badly to yourself—for example, "I always mess up"—this is called negative self-talk and is a withdrawal from your self-esteem piggy bank. It is important to learn how to recognize negative self-talk and to understand that there are actions that can be taken to make this talk you have in your head more positive.

Use the following example:

You are playing with your friend Shan after school. You have had a bad day at school because you fell over and grazed your knee at lunchtime, and a group of older students laughed at you. You are not being a lot of fun. Shan starts to play with another group of students, leaving you alone. You feel hurt that she is playing with someone else.

What can you say to yourself to make yourself feel better?

"Shan has gone to play with another group not because she doesn't like me anymore, but because she does not understand that my knee hurts and that I don't feel like playing today. Tomorrow I will tell her that I really like playing with her and why I couldn't play with her."

Following the discussion about positive and negative self-talk, ask students to write positive self-talk statements on their bandages and stick them on their clothes. To help students think of more ideas, encourage them to read the bandages stuck on other students.

Teacher note: For some students, it may be better to create a larger bandage template instead of using regular bandages to write messages.

Developing Key Messages

Activity—Poster

Supply each student with a piece of art paper. Explain that each student is going to create an advertising poster for an imaginary first aid kit for times when he or she might feel sad and has hurt feelings. The kit will help remind students to focus on what's good to help take away the pain and repair their hurt feelings. Students compile a list of objects they could include in their first aid kit.

The kit could include:

- Happy bandages with positive messages
- Caring cream
- Feel better powder
- Supportive gauze

Students choose one item from the kit and then write and illustrate how and why this object will help them feel better. Display advertisements around the classroom as a reminder to students that there are positive actions they can all take to help themselves feel better when their feelings are hurt. Share the following sample poster suggestion with students.

Huggables Supportive Gauze

If you are feeling sad, use our new supportive gauze. Just like a great big hug, it wraps all around you and holds you tight.

Instructions for use: Have a friend or family member wrap the gauze around you so his or her arms encircle you, and stay like this for a few minutes or until you start to feel better.

Reflecting on Key Messages

Student Journal

Students list situations that would make them feel hurt and record positive actions they could take to make themselves feel better.

Teacher Reflection

How effectively were the key messages developed?

To what extent are your students now able to:

- Describe situations that may hurt their feelings?
- Identify positive actions they can take when their feelings are hurt?
- Demonstrate ways to help themselves feel better?

Section 2

Focus 4: Safe or Unsafe Feelings

Key Messages

Our body gives us clues that tell us we are safe.

Our body sends us warning signals to let us know that we might not be in a safe situation.

This focus will enable students to:

- Identify feelings that help them recognize when they are safe
- Identify feelings that warn them they are not in a safe situation
- Describe when and where they feel safe and unsafe at school
- Demonstrate when they need to ask an adult for help
- Use strategies to keep themselves safe in social situations

Focus 4 Activities	Resources Needed
Introducing Key Messages	
Literature	*The Three Little Pigs* (Halliwell, 1886) or *Three Billy Goats Gruff* (Dasent, 1859)
Mapping our thoughts	Chart paper, markers
Developing Key Messages	
Mapping safe actions at school	Maps of the school, sticky notes, writing materials
Reflecting on Key Messages	
Journal	Journal, drawing materials, glue

Introducing Key Messages

Literature

Read students the story *The Three Little Pigs* (Halliwell, 1886), and discuss how the pigs felt when the wolf threatened to blow their houses down.

Or, alternatively:

Read students the story *Three Billy Goats Gruff* (Dasent, 1859), and discuss how the Troll tried to make the three goats feel unsafe as they tried to cross the bridge. Ask the students to think about how Little Billy Goat Gruff would have felt when the Troll first tried to scare him off the bridge. Discuss how bodies can react when you feel afraid—trembling, shaking, feeling breathless, and heart racing. Ask the students to play charades in which they mime situations where they might feel safe and unsafe. Students guess what these situations are.

Discuss the following questions.

- How do you feel when someone yells at you?
- How do you feel when someone speaks kindly to you?
- How can you tell the difference between friendly and unfriendly behavior?

Activity—Mapping Our Thoughts

Create a large chart divided into two columns for students as follows.

I feel safe when . . .	I feel unsafe when . . .

Ask the students to think about when they feel safe and unsafe at school. Record each situation on the appropriate list. Look at the list of unsafe situations, and discuss what students could do if they found themselves in one of these situations. Remind the students to ask for help when they feel unsafe or unsure of what to do.

Discuss the actions students could take in the following situations.

- A lady you don't know asks you to get into her car in the parking lot after school.
- An older student tells you to hand over your lunch money or else you will get punched really hard.
- A student tries to push you off the monkey bars.
- You are attacked by a bird on the playground.

Section 2

Developing Key Messages

Activity—Mapping Safe Actions at School

Divide students into pairs, and give each pair a map of the school. Using this map, students mark places where they feel safe and unsafe. Project a large map of the school on a wall, using PowerPoint or SMART Board, and ask students to write on sticky notes the actions they have brainstormed to improve how safe students feel in each of these areas. As a whole class, students attach their sticky notes to the large map and describe the actions they recommend to the rest of the class. Some examples of safe actions include:

- Staying in the areas of the playground where they are meant to play
- Making sure they can always see a teacher or know where to find one if they need help
- Avoiding playing on dangerous equipment or in dangerous ways (students can suggest examples)
- Staying away from other students who are not being nice
- Staying with their friends
- Asking someone to go to the bathroom or the cafeteria with them at recess or lunchtime
- Not talking to people they don't know unless a teacher or their parents say it is OK

Reflecting on Key Messages

Student Journal

Students draw what they think their friendly face looks like to others and paste this picture in their journals.

Teacher Reflection

How effectively were the key messages developed?

To what extent are your students now able to:

- Identify feelings that help them recognize when they are safe?
- Identify feelings that warn them they are not in a safe situation?
- Describe when and where they feel safe and unsafe at school?
- Demonstrate when they need to ask an adult for help?
- Use strategies to keep themselves safe in social situations?

Chapter 10

Self-Management

Emotional Regulation, Resilience, and Self-Motivation

THE "CHINA SHOP INCIDENT" HAD BEEN A REAL TURNING POINT FOR BUSBY, FORCING HIM TO REFLECT ON THE IMPACT OF HIS BEHAVIOUR ON OTHERS.

Self-management skills enable us to control and direct our emotions in appropriate ways. This involves:

- Managing our emotions so they don't stop us from effectively dealing with situations and pursuing our goals
- Striving to achieve our goals despite difficulties

Key Area 2: Self-Management

Focus	This Focus Will Enable Students to:	Focus Activities
1. Managing our feelings	• Explain why it is important to learn to manage their feelings • Describe the positive and negative ways in which their bodies can react to feelings • Demonstrate ways of managing their feelings	• Literature • Fast-tracking good feelings • Writing • Journal
2. Positive thinking	• Identify factors that can spoil a good day • Demonstrate positive actions they can take to turn a not-so-good day into a better day • Identify self-talk that can make them feel better about themselves	• Literature • Brainstorm • Writing: Flat and dented • Journal
3. Perseverance	• Define perseverance • Describe situations where perseverance is needed • Demonstrate an ability to persevere in challenging situations	• Literature • Quote study • Perseverance sayings • Journal

Key Area 2: Self-Management

Emotional Regulation, Resilience, and Self-Motivation

Focus 1: Managing Our Feelings

Key Messages

There are strategies we can use to manage how we are feeling.

Talking with someone we trust when we are not feeling good can help us feel better.

This focus will enable students to:

- Explain why it is important to learn to manage their feelings
- Describe the positive and negative ways in which their bodies can react to feelings
- Demonstrate ways of managing their feelings

Focus 1 Activities	Resources Needed
Introducing Key Messages	
Literature	A text that provides an example of how our body can react negatively to some feelings (Sample text: *When I'm Feeling Jealous* by Trace Moroney, 2007)
Developing Key Messages	
Fast-tracking good feelings	Large sheets of paper, writing and drawing materials
Writing	Paper, writing materials
Reflecting on Key Messages	
Journal	Journal, writing materials

Introducing Key Messages

Sometimes it can be hard to tell someone that we're feeling sad, worried, or upset, but talking about our feelings is important. If we keep these feelings to ourselves and don't talk about them, they can make us feel even worse. Talking to someone who cares about you will help you start feeling better. Although our worries don't always disappear right away, it does help to express the way we feel, and the person we tell can help us find ways to deal with these feelings.

It can also be difficult to recognize when our feelings are becoming out of control. Brainstorm how we can tell when this is happening to us and what some of the obvious signs are, such as talking louder, going red in the face, stamping feet, clenching fists, feeling your heart racing, or lashing out at others. Sharing your feelings with someone you trust can give you support and even ideas for actions that can be taken to help to get your feelings under control.

Emotions students could monitor include anxiety, anger, jealousy, and fear. Discuss the following questions for whichever emotion is being monitored.

- Why is it important to monitor how we are feeling? How does knowing this help us feel better?
- What information can we gather by monitoring other class members' emotions?

Literature

Choose and read a text that provides an example of how our bodies can react negatively to some feelings.

The following example uses jealousy as the focus for discussion. Other feelings can be substituted depending on the feeling that was the focus in the chosen text.

Share with students a story about a time you felt jealous and how it made you feel. An example could be that when you were little your grandparents gave you and your siblings a boogie board each. Yours was much smaller, and you felt jealous of your siblings and secretly hoped their boogie boards would break. When you went to the beach you had such fun on your new board you felt sorry about the way you had felt.

Ask students to recall a time when they felt jealous of something or someone, and ask them to describe how they felt. List responses on the whiteboard, and beside each, write something students could say or do to help them feel less jealous. For example, "I felt jealous of the birthday presents my friend received but told myself when it was my birthday I would receive some great presents too."

Example Using *When I'm Feeling Jealous* by Trace Moroney (2007)

This story is about a little rabbit that feels jealous for lots of reasons but does not like the way this makes him feel inside. The rabbit decides to try and come up with some ways he could change this feeling.

Developing Key Messages

Activity—Fast-Tracking Good Feelings

Sometimes for no particular reason, we find that we feel out of sorts, and this can affect how good we are feeling about lots of things. There are actions we can take to feel better and get our feelings back under control. Arrange students in small groups, and allocate each group one of the following feelings and objectives (Elkind+Swert Communications, n.d.).

- I am feeling bored. I would like to feel more enthusiastic.
- I am feeling worried. I would like to feel more laid-back.
- I am feeling afraid. I would like to feel safer.
- I am feeling sad. I would like to feel happier.
- I am feeling angry. I would like to feel calmer.
- I am feeling nervous. I would like to feel more relaxed.
- I am feeling jealous. I would like to feel happy for other people when they have something I don't.

Ask each group to brainstorm actions students could take to help themselves feel more positive for the emotion their group is allocated. Students write or draw all their ideas on a large sheet of paper. They then discuss their ideas and decide which positive emotions would work best for them. Encourage each group to share its ideas with the rest of the class.

Activity—Writing

Before we tell others how we feel, we should try to understand what those feelings are like and when we may feel this way. On a sheet of paper, ask students to record some of the feelings they have experienced during the last week. A good way to do this is to think of something that has happened to them and how it made them feel.

In pairs, ask students to discuss the feelings they have recorded and to write a few short sentences about when they experienced the feeling, how strong it was, and what effect it had on them. They should then write about how they made, or could have made, this emotion more positive. This activity will allow students to build a framework around their feelings and help them understand why they sometimes feel the way they do and what they can do to help them deal with these emotions more positively. Students can paste these ideas in their journals.

Section 2

Reflecting on Key Messages

Student Journal

Ask each student to think about the ideas collected during the last activity and to decide and write about the ones that would work best for him or her. Students could try using the following format.

"If I am feeling sad, and I would like to feel better, I could try . . ."

Teacher Reflection

How effectively were the key messages developed?

To what extent are your students now able to:

- Explain why it is important to learn to manage their feelings?
- Describe the positive and negative ways in which their bodies can react to feelings?
- Demonstrate ways of managing their feelings?

Focus 2: Positive Thinking

Key Messages

We all have days when nothing seems to go right.

On these days, there are actions we can take to make ourselves feel better.

We all have bad days sometimes, when things just seem to always be going wrong or things just seem to be all bad. This happens to everyone at some time, and there are things we can do to make ourselves feel better.

This focus will enable students to:

- Identify factors that can spoil a good day
- Demonstrate positive actions they can take to turn a not-so-good day into a better day
- Identify self-talk that can make them feel better about themselves

Focus 2 Activities	Resources Needed
Introducing Key Messages	
Literature and discussion	A text that provides an example of having a bad day (Sample text: *Alexander and the Terrible, Horrible, No Good, Very Bad Day* by Judith Viorst, 1987)
Developing Key Messages	
Brainstorm	Paper, writing materials
Writing—Flat and dented	Balloons, felt-tip pens
Reflecting on Key Messages	
Journal	Journal, writing materials

Section 2

Introducing Key Messages

Literature

Choose a text that provides an example of having a bad day.

Before Reading

Explain to students that sometimes we all have bad days when things just seem to be going wrong. This can happen to everyone at some point in time, but there are things we can do to make ourselves feel better.

Read the text, and conduct a guided discussion to identify the different feelings.

- Why was _____ having a bad day?
- How did this character feel when things started to go wrong?
- What happened to make him or her feel better?

Discuss with students how the way we feel about ourselves can affect the way we react to and manage situations. When we feel good about ourselves we are able to cope better, have confidence to try new things, and are able to make better choices.

Brainstorm with students some situations that affect how we feel and how our feelings can affect the way we look. For example, a student may feel nervous when returning to school after a new haircut. Have students brainstorm and role-play how people look when they don't feel good about themselves.

For example:

Feeling not-so-good looks like:

- Limp celery—Droopy and miserable
- Jiggling tea bag—Nervous and wriggly
- Prickly cactus—Grumpy and angry

Feeling good looks like:

- Eiffel Tower—Stands tall
- Melting marshmallow—Looks relaxed
- Cheshire cat—Smiles and looks confident

Example Using *Alexander and the Terrible, Horrible, No Good, Very Bad Day* by Judith Viorst (2007)

Alexander gets out of bed to find bubble gum in his hair. Before he's even left the house, he trips on his skateboard and drops his sweater in the sink. He can already tell it's going to be a bad day. The string of unfortunate events continues, but when he resolves to move to Australia his mother helps him put things into perspective.

After Reading

Discuss the story and how Alexander felt. Talk about how Alexander found ways to express his feelings and how this made him feel.

Developing Key Messages

Activity—Brainstorm

Ask the students to think about and discuss what people who feel good and not-so-good might say about themselves. How would these people feel when they say these things? Arrange students into groups, and give each group a large sheet of paper. Ask each group to draw a line down the middle of the sheet to create a chart with "Feel Not-So-Good" statements on one side and "Feel Good" statements on the other.

For example:

Feel Not-So-Good	Feel Good
I feel miserable because I am useless.	I feel nervous, but I know I'll be fine.
I feel worried that nobody likes me.	I feel afraid, but I know I can handle this situation.
I feel angry that I will never get on the team.	
I feel scared that everyone will laugh at me.	I feel disappointed, but I know I will do better next time.
I feel it's my fault.	I feel worried, but I know that if I just be myself and be friendly I will make friends.

Ask students to share their statements, and ask how they felt when they were writing each list.

- Have they ever said those sorts of things to themselves?
- Did it feel better writing the feel-good statements?

Teacher note: People with high self-esteem might still have the same feelings of fear or worry, but they deal with these differently. When our self-talk is positive, we convince ourselves we are able to deal with the situation. If our self-talk is negative, we behave in a negative way and feel that we can't cope.

Activity—Writing: Flat and Dented

Inflate a balloon, and draw a happy, smiling face on it. Ask students to imagine you have drawn this face because you are enjoying the day and have just finished building an amazing castle with building blocks. Deflate the balloon a little, and explain to students that you are feeling a little flat and dented because your sibling has knocked over the building block castle you took hours to build. Deflate the balloon a little further, and explain that you are feeling angry because some of the pieces have fallen through a hole in the wooden floor. Ask students to suggest what you could do to feel less angry. For example, you could ask your dad to help you get the missing pieces back and suggest your sibling help rebuild the castle.

Supply each student with a balloon and felt-tip pen, and ask students to draw a happy face on the balloon.

Ask students to identify and write about situations that might cause someone to get a dent or to feel flat. Discuss how during these times we might not be feeling so good about ourselves. If we are feeling sad and down, we could be more easily upset. If we are feeling angry and grumpy, we would also be easy to upset. People who bully often bully people who look like easy targets to get a reaction. If they can upset someone and that person shows he or she is upset, they will probably try to upset that person again. Invite students to share their writing with the class, using their balloon to demonstrate how they were feeling at each step of the story. Explain to students that each story is to finish with a suggestion of positive thoughts or actions they can take to reinflate their balloon.

Reflecting on Key Messages

Student Journal

Have students think of a time when they have felt not-so-good about themselves, and encourage them to write about it (if they feel comfortable doing so).

- What did it feel like?
- Was your self-talk positive or negative? What did you say to yourself?
- What might you do differently now if the same thing happened?
- What have you learned about how to make yourself feel better?

Teacher Reflection

How effectively were the key messages developed?

To what extent are your students now able to:

- Identify factors that can spoil a good day?
- Demonstrate positive actions they can take to turn a not-so-good day into a better day?
- Identify self-talk that can make them feel better about themselves?

Focus 3: Perseverance

Key Messages

We all face challenges, and sometimes these seem impossible to get through.

Perseverance means believing in what you are doing and working hard to achieve your goal, even when it seems as if you might never get there.

This focus will enable students to:

- Define perseverance
- Describe situations in which perseverance is needed
- Demonstrate an ability to persevere in challenging situations

Focus 3 Activities	Resources Needed
Introducing Key Messages	
Literature and discussion	A text that provides an example of perseverance (Sample texts: *When Pigs Fly* by Valerie Coulman, 2001, or *The Little Engine That Could* by Watty Piper, 1990)
Developing Key Messages	
Quote study	Paper, drawing and writing materials
Perseverance sayings	Paper, drawing and collage materials
Reflecting on Key Messages	
Journal	Journal, drawing and writing materials

Section 2

Introducing Key Messages

Literature

Choose and read a text that provides an example of perseverance. Initiate a class discussion using the following questions.

- When have you tried something new or something that was hard to do?
- Was it easy or hard?
- Did you stop or keep going?
- What made you keep trying?
- After reading this story, do you want to try again?
- What do you think you can do now to succeed or to reach your goal?
- What could help you persevere more at a task? (For example, *feeling success*)

Example Using *When Pigs Fly* by Valerie Coulman (2001)

Ralph the cow desperately wants a bicycle. His father, who can't imagine a cow doing such a thing, tells him he will get him a bike when pigs fly. Ralph, undaunted, searches for a way to get pigs airborne.

Example Using *The Little Engine That Could* by Watty Piper (1990)

A little steam engine must pull her train over a steep hill. She can't do it by herself, so she searches for another engine to help her. While the big engines all refuse, an equally small engine cheerfully agrees, and together they haul their cars up and over the hill, repeating the mantra "I think I can, I think I can."

After Reading

Discuss with students how difficult it can be to persevere sometimes, and also discuss the great sense of achievement you feel when you do complete what you considered to be an almost impossible task. In pairs, ask students to relate to their partner a time when they were in this position, such as running in a cross-country event, learning to fly a kite, or finishing a project like building a toy that takes some time to complete, and to describe what helped them keep trying and be determined to complete their task. Invite selected students to share their stories with the rest of the class.

Developing Key Messages

Activity—Quote Study

Try, Try, Try Again

Many people in history have done amazing things that were thought to be impossible. Without their perseverance, amazing inventions, incredible structures, and creative arts might never have been developed, and athletic records might never have been broken.

Consider the following quote.

"I never failed once when I invented the lightbulb. It just happened to be a two-thousand-step process."—Thomas Edison

- How would our lives be different if Thomas Edison hadn't decided to persevere with the task of inventing lightbulbs?
- What does this quote tell us about the importance of positive thinking?

One answer could be that not being able to do something doesn't mean I have failed, it just means the task is difficult. I'll get there if I keep trying.

Discuss the following quotes and what they mean.

"It's not that I'm so smart, it's just that I stay with problems longer."—Albert Einstein

"Be like a postage stamp, stick to something until you get there!" —Josh Billings

Students, individually or in pairs, can write and illustrate their own quote about persevering.

These quotes can be displayed around the school and a short explanation of this activity can be given by selected class members at a school assembly.

Activity—Perseverance Sayings

Explain to students one way of helping to persevere with something is to have a reminder to help you achieve your goal. Some people may invent a saying like "I can do this" or "I just need to try a bit harder and I will get there" to repeat to themselves if they ever feel like giving up. Others might like something they can look at, for example, a badge or a magnet. Give each student a piece of paper folded in half horizontally. Ask students to create a saying suitable for a badge or magnet that would help them persevere with a task. Explain to the students that they can take their creations home, pin them on their shirt, or put them on their fridge. When they see a friend or family member display perseverance, they can loan them their saying for a day. These sayings could be created as badges or magnets, time and resources permitting.

Reflecting on Key Messages

Student Journal

Ask students to illustrate and write about a time when they were tempted to give up on a project they were working on or a skill they were trying to perfect. Remind students to write about the strategies they found useful to help them complete their task or what they could do next time to complete the task. For example, who could they get help from to encourage them to complete the task?

Teacher Reflection

How effectively were the key messages developed?

To what extent are your students now able to:

- Define perseverance?
- Describe situations in which perseverance is needed?
- Demonstrate an ability to persevere in challenging situations?

Chapter 11

Social Awareness

Understanding and Interpreting Social Situations

Social awareness skills help us to be aware and respectful of the feelings and perspectives of others. This involves:

- Recognizing what others may be feeling
- Trying to understand a situation from another's point of view
- Accepting and valuing people who are different from ourselves

Key Area 3: Social Awareness

Focus	This Focus Will Enable Students to:	Focus Activities
1. Giving—Making deposits	• Identify the value of giving to and sharing with others • Describe how their friendly behaviors—taking turns, sharing, speaking in a friendly way, listening to others' ideas, and caring about others and their feelings—can lead to positive feelings for themselves • Demonstrate ways to develop and maintain positive friendship groups using their friendly behaviors	• Literature • Brainstorm • Narrative writing—If I had . . . • Quiz—How friendly are you? • Journal
2. Making things better	• Identify times when they or others are not being treated nicely • Describe what someone can do to feel better when being treated unkindly • Demonstrate ways to feel better when treated unkindly	• Think, pair, share • Turning withdrawals into deposits • Literature • Journal

Key Area 3: Social Awareness

Understanding and Interpreting Social Situations

Focus 1: Giving—Making Deposits

Key Messages

The way we think, feel, and act shows people we care about them and value them in our lives.

This focus will enable students to:

- Identify the value of giving to and sharing with others
- Describe how their friendly behaviors—taking turns, sharing, speaking in a friendly way, listening to others' ideas, and caring about others and their feelings—can lead to positive feelings for themselves
- Demonstrate ways to develop and maintain positive friendship groups using their friendly behaviors

Focus 1 Activities	Resources Needed
Introducing Key Messages	
Literature	A text that provides an example of being thoughtful and caring toward others
	(Sample text: *The Gift: A Hanukkah Story* by Aliana Brodmann, 1998)
Brainstorm	Paper, drawing and writing materials
Developing Key Messages	
Narrative writing—If I had . . .	Writing materials
Quiz—How friendly are you?	Paper, pens
Reflecting on Key Messages	
Journal	Journal, writing materials

Section 2

Introducing Key Messages

There are many things we do that help others to feel better. When you first meet someone, he or she needs to know that you are friendly. You can show people that you are friendly with a gesture, a smile, saying hello and introducing yourself, or by doing something nice for them.

Doing something for someone else can also make you feel good. Caring for and helping others makes them feel good and is a great way to make you feel good too.

Literature

Choose and read a text that provides an example of being thoughtful and caring toward others. Conduct a guided discussion to identify the behaviors shown in the story and the effect they had on others.

Example Using *The Gift: A Hanukkah Story* by Aliana Brodmann (1998)

A little girl goes shopping with her Hanukkah money, hoping to buy herself a special gift. But she can't decide what to get until the lovely music from a street musician catches her ear. She donates her money to the musician and realizes that giving is just as good as receiving.

Discuss the lesson learned from this story about unselfishly giving to others and unexpectedly receiving something for yourself.

Activity—Brainstorm

Arrange the students into groups, and ask them to brainstorm responses to the following question.

If you had $50 what could you do to help someone else that might make a difference in his or her life and make you feel really good as well? Have the students record their answers on a big sheet of paper and then later share these with the class.

Developing Key Messages

Activity—Narrative Writing: If I Had . . .

Using one of the ideas from the last activity, ask the students to write a narrative story about what they would do to help someone else if they were given $100. Remind students to write about how they felt about giving and what they got in return for their kind act.

Activity—Quiz: How Friendly Are You?

Discuss the qualities of a friend. Explain to the students that the class is going to prepare a "friendly" interview. Ask each student to create a question he or she believes would measure how friendly someone is, for example:

If you find a person who has fallen over at school, do you . . .

    a)   Show you care by smiling sympathetically?

    b)   Ask if you can help?

    c)   Make fun of him or her for falling over?

    d)   Go and tell the teacher on duty?

Collect the questions and combine common ones, using the remaining questions to create a class interview sheet called "How Friendly Are You?" Encourage students to interview at least three other students in their class and two adults. Students summarize and share their findings about the friendly qualities they observed and briefly explain how they think these qualities can help improve friendships.

Reflecting on Key Messages

Student Journal

After completing the quiz, have students complete the following sentences on a page in their journal.

I show friendly behaviors when I . . .

I could be friendlier by . . .

Teacher Reflection

How effectively were the key messages developed?

To what extent are your students now able to:

- Identify the value of giving to and sharing with others?
- Describe how their friendly behaviors—taking turns, sharing, speaking in a friendly way, listening to others' ideas, and caring about others and their feelings—can lead to positive feelings for themselves?
- Demonstrate ways to develop and maintain positive friendship groups using their friendly behaviors?

Section 2

Focus 2: Making Things Better

Key Messages

When you are not being treated nicely by others, there are actions you can take to help yourself feel better.

This focus will enable students to:

- Identify times when they or others are not being treated nicely
- Describe what someone can do to feel better when being treated unkindly
- Demonstrate ways to feel better when treated unkindly

Focus 2 Activities	Resources Needed
Introducing Key Messages	
Think, pair, share	Paper, writing materials
Turning withdrawals into deposits	
Developing Key Messages	
Literature	A text that provides an example of unkind behavior (Sample text: *Enemy Pie* by Derek Munson, 2000)
Reflecting on Key Messages	
Journal	Journal, writing materials

Introducing Key Messages

Sometimes people can be mean and uncaring, such as when bullying and teasing. People who do this hurt others and are usually not liked by many.

Activity—Think, Pair, Share

In pairs, ask students to brainstorm examples of negative behaviors that would hurt or cause withdrawals from a person's emotional piggy bank, such as teasing, leaving someone out, name calling, spreading rumors, or being mean. Collate and make a list of behaviors to avoid in your classroom.

Now encourage students to make a list of positive friendly behaviors that would make others feel better (deposits into our emotional piggy banks), such as helping, sharing, caring about others, asking others to join in, or helping new people.

Discussion—Turning Withdrawals Into Deposits

Explain to the students that when someone is being mean to them and making withdrawals from their emotional piggy banks so that they feel upset, it usually will not make them feel better to be mean back. Discuss how it can often make matters worse.

Developing Key Messages

Literature

Choose and read a text that provides an example of unkind behavior. Initiate a class discussion using the following questions:

- Why did the character choose to behave in an unkind way?
- How did the unkind behaviors impact others?
- What would you have done in this situation?

Example Using *Enemy Pie* by Derek Munson (2000)

A boy's summer is ruined by his new neighbor, Jeremy Ross. Jeremy laughs at him when he strikes out in softball and invites everyone but him to a trampoline party. Jeremy is quickly placed on top of the boy's enemy list. His father proposes that they make and feed Jeremy "enemy pie." The catch is the boy must spend a whole day being nice to Jeremy to convince him to eat the pie. After a day of hanging out the boy finds Jeremy isn't so bad after all, and surprisingly the enemy pie that his father made is delicious.

After reading, discuss with the students:

- Why did the main character think Jeremy Ross was his enemy?
- Did the enemy pie work the way the main character thought it would? Why or why not?
- What does the story tell us about deciding we don't like someone without getting to know him or her first?
- What could you do if you met someone like Jeremy Ross?

Reflecting on Key Messages

Student Journal

Students illustrate a situation that involves unkind behavior. Insert a speech bubble or thinking cloud to show what the people involved could do or say to feel better.

Teacher Reflection

How effectively were the key messages developed?

To what extent are your students now able to:

- Identify times when they or others are not being treated nicely?
- Describe what someone can do to feel better when being treated unkindly?
- Demonstrate ways to feel better when treated unkindly?

Chapter 12

Relationship Skills

Positive Relationship Skills

Relationship skills help us deal with relationship problems and other social conflicts. These skills include:

- Making friends and maintaining healthy relationships
- Dealing effectively with negative social influences and conflicts
- Seeking help if we are not able to solve a social problem ourselves

Key Area 4: Relationship Skills

Focus	This Focus Will Enable Students to:	Focus Activities
1. Bullying behaviors	• Describe the characteristics of specific types of bullying behavior • Predict whether a behavior is bullying or not bullying • Demonstrate the ability to distinguish between and respond to bullying and nonbullying behaviors	• Literature • Is this bullying? • Types of bullying • What type of bullying is this? • Journal
2. Bullying—Keeping safe	• Identify if a behavior is bullying or not bullying • Describe ways to assess potential risks before responding to a bullying situation • Demonstrate safe actions to take as a bystander to a bullying situation	• Risk-o-Meter • Is this situation harmful? • Journal
3. How does it feel to be bullied?	• Identify feelings others may experience as a result of being bullied • Describe the possible physical and mental effects of bullying behavior • Demonstrate actions they can take to discourage bullying behavior	• Literature • Graffiti • Literature and discussion • Being bullied—How does it feel, and what can you do about it? • Journal

Key Area 4: Relationship Skills

Positive Relationship Skills

Focus 1: Bullying Behaviors

Key Messages

Some behavior can be unkind and wrong but is not always bullying.

Bullying is when someone means to hurt or upset someone else again and again.

Bullying behavior is not tolerated in our friendly school.

This focus will enable students to:

- Describe the characteristics of specific types of bullying behavior
- Predict whether a behavior is bullying or not bullying
- Demonstrate the ability to distinguish between and respond to bullying and nonbullying behaviors

Focus 1 Activities	Resources Needed
Introducing Key Messages	
Literature	A text that provides an example of bullying behavior (Sample text: *The Recess Queen* by Alexis O'Neill, 2002)
Is this bullying?	Two containers, felt-tip pens, laminated cards made from resource sheet: "Is This Bullying?"
Types of bullying	Resource sheet: "Types of Bullying"
Developing Key Messages	
What type of bullying is this?	Resource sheet: "Types of Bullying" Masking tape, precut pieces of card, writing material
Reflecting on Key Messages	
Journal	Journal, writing materials

Section 2

Introducing Key Messages

Literature

Choose and read a text that provides an example of bullying behavior. Discuss the behavior and the effect it had on others.

Ask the students to brainstorm behaviors they believe are examples of bullying and discuss why they identified these behaviors. Record the behaviors on the board. Alternatively, ask each student to construct a Y chart, which is a chart divided into three sections in the shape of a *Y*. Students use the Y chart by filling out one section about what bullying looks like, one section to show examples of what bullying sounds like, and the final section to indicate what bullying feels like.

Ask the students to review the behaviors they have listed as bullying based on this definition. Combine all ideas on one large class Y chart and display. Explain to the students that how the target of the bullying behavior feels is related to whether a situation is bullying or not. For example, if a friend is teasing you, and you feel that it is not mean but just fun, then it is not bullying. If the person intended to hurt someone or someone felt hurt by repeated nasty behaviors then this is considered to be bullying.

Example Using *The Recess Queen* by Alexis O'Neill (2002)

Mean Jean was the recess queen. When the recess bell sounded, she had first rights on all the playground equipment, and nobody dared to say differently. That is, until the diminutive Katie Sue arrives.

Activity—Is This Bullying?

Prepare a class set of laminated situation cards using the resource sheet "Is This Bullying?" Have two containers available into which students can place their answers; one labeled "Bullying Behavior," and the other "Not Bullying Behavior." In groups of three, students take turns to read the situation cards, discuss, and decide in which container to place the card. Discuss with the students why some choices may have been difficult, and ask them to describe what they did as a group to help decide in which container to place the situations. Provide felt-tip pens for students to write their own scenarios on the blank cards provided. Put the container with the bullying situations aside for the next activity.

Activity—Types of Bullying

Show students the "Types of Bullying" resource sheet and discuss. Explain that when people think about bullying they often only think of physical bullying, such as hitting or pushing. Discuss how there is a range of other behaviors that bullies use to try to make another person scared or upset. Explain to students it can be helpful to consider the following questions when faced with a bullying situation and not knowing how to respond.

- What is the other person doing?
- Is he or she behaving this way to deliberately hurt me?
- Has this person tried to hurt me before?
- How do I feel about his or her behavior?
- Is this bullying?
- Am I likely to get hurt?
- What should I do next?

Developing Key Messages

Activity—What Type of Bullying Is This?

Using wide masking tape, construct a grid on the classroom floor or in the outside undercover area with headings corresponding to the subheadings in the "Types of Bullying" resource sheet (see the following example).

Distribute precut pieces of card to each student. Ask the students to write a brief sentence describing both offline and online behavior they would classify as bullying, for example:

- *One student jabs another in the back with a ruler to deliberately hurt him every day (offline).*
- *A student is telling lies about someone in an email (online).*

Suggestions placed in the container during the earlier discussion should be included in this activity. Remind the students not to use classmates' names when writing their sentences.

Ask the students to place all the strips of cardboard into the container labeled "bullying behavior." Students take turns drawing one card from the container, reading it to the rest of the class, and then placing it on the grid. Students respond using thumbs up or thumbs down whether they agree or disagree with the placement. If they disagree, an explanation needs to be given and the card moved to the correct column. Discuss how some forms of bullying can be classified under several headings, such as telling lies about someone in an email.

Exclusion	Physical	Lies or Rumors	Verbal Abuse and Teasing	Cyber

Section 2

Reflecting on Key Messages

Student Journal

Students choose one of the types of bullying as identified on the "Types of Bullying" resource sheet. Record an example of this type of bullying and a positive action that could be taken in response to the bullying behavior. Provide an opportunity to share with a partner or small group.

Teacher Reflection

How effectively were the key messages developed?

To what extent are your students now able to:

- Describe the characteristics of specific types of bullying behavior?
- Predict whether a behavior is bullying or not bullying?
- Demonstrate the ability to distinguish between and respond to bullying and nonbullying behaviors?

Focus 2: Bullying—Keeping Safe

Key Messages

When we see someone being bullied we may not know what to do to help him or her.

We should always assess the risks to ourselves and others before we respond to bullying.

This focus will enable students to:

- Identify if a behavior is bullying or not bullying
- Describe ways to assess potential risks before responding to a bullying situation
- Demonstrate safe actions to take as a bystander to a bullying situation

Focus 2 Activities	Resources Needed
Introducing Key Messages	
Risk-o-Meter	Activity sheet: "Risk-o-Meter"
	Colored pens and pencils, brass fastener or mounting putty
Developing Key Messages	
Is this situation harmful?	Resource sheet: "Is This Situation Harmful?"
	Resource sheet: "Is This Bullying?"
Reflecting on Key Messages	
Journal	Journal, writing materials

Section 2

Introducing Key Messages

When you see someone or a group being bullied and want to do something to make it stop, first you need to decide if it is safe for you to help. If the situation is not safe, you need to know who to go to for help and where to find that person. The roles that emerge in a bullying situation are the following.

- *A person who bullies (ringleader):* This person intentionally tries to hurt another person.

- *A person who is being bullied:* This person is deliberately made to feel fear and distress or is physically or emotionally hurt by a more powerful person or group and is unable to stop it from happening.

- *Bystander:* This person sees the bullying or knows that it is happening to someone else. There may be bystanders who are afraid they may be bullied next, and this may influence their decision about what they will do if they see bullying happening. There are different types of bystanders as follows:

  - *Contributor:* These people offer support to the person bullying, either by helping the person to bully the other person or by encouraging the person bullying. This group might gather to watch the incident (sometimes from concern for the person being bullied, sometimes to see what will happen, and sometimes for enjoyment).

  - *Supporter:* People that fall into this group dislike the bullying and do not actively help the person bullying. This group is concerned for the person being bullied and actively tries to help the person being bullied.

- *Witness:* This person knows the bullying is going on but is not directly involved.

Activity—Risk-o-Meter

Ask students to look at the "Risk-o-Meter" activity sheet and explain how the Risk-o-Meter works. It ranges from minimal harm, to moderate harm, to extreme harm. The harm refers to what harm might come to a student as a consequence of responding as a bystander to a bullying situation. Relate this to the flaggers students may have seen on roadsides to warn of a potential road hazard.

Ask students to color the Risk-o-Meter in the colors described on the activity sheet.

- Very low—Light green
- Low—Light blue
- Moderate—Yellow
- High—Light orange
- Very high—Dark orange
- Extreme—Red

Give students a template of the arrow, or ask students to cut the arrow from the sheet and attach it to their Risk-o-Meter with a brass fastener or mounting putty so the arrow can be moved on its axis.

Developing Key Messages

Activity—Is This Situation Harmful?

Read each of the situations on the "Is This Situation Harmful?" resource sheet. Refer students to questions on the "Is This Bullying?" resource sheet.

- What is the other person doing?
- Is he or she behaving this way to deliberately hurt me?
- Has this person tried to hurt me before?
- How do I feel about his or her behavior?
- Is this bullying?
- Am I likely to get hurt?
- What should I do next?

Arrange the class into small groups, and ask the students to discuss the level of potential harm they think they might experience as a bystander in each scenario and to move the arrow on the Risk-o-Meter accordingly. For example, "This is a bullying situation, and the student doing the bullying is much bigger than me and I feel frightened. The chance of getting hurt or being in danger is very high."

Based on where students place the arrow, students discuss what action they could take to help without putting themselves in danger. Students can write their own scenarios in the blank boxes provided.

Reflecting on Key Messages

Student Journal

Ask students to describe a bullying situation they have seen or been involved in.

- What type of bullying was it?
- How did it make you feel?
- What did you do?
- How did you feel about the person who bullied another student?
- What would you do if this happened again?

Teacher Reflection

How effectively were the key messages developed?

To what extent are your students now able to:

- Identify if a behavior is bullying or not bullying?
- Describe ways to assess potential risks before responding to a bullying situation?
- Demonstrate safe actions to take as a bystander to a bullying situation?

Section 2

Focus 3: How Does It Feel to Be Bullied?

Key Messages

When a person who is bullied is shown care, respect, and understanding by bystanders he or she feels supported and is usually better able to cope with the situation.

Positive bystanders help send a clear message to people who bully that their behavior is not acceptable and should stop.

This focus will enable students to:

- Identify feelings others may experience as a result of being bullied
- Describe the possible physical and mental effects of bullying behavior
- Demonstrate actions they can take to discourage bullying behavior

Focus 3 Activities	Resources Needed
Introducing Key Messages	
Literature	A text that provides an example of how bullying can make a person feel (Sample text: *King of the Playground* by Phyllis Reynolds Naylor, 1994)
Graffiti	Paper, drawing materials
Developing Key Messages	
Literature	Resource sheet: "New Boy "
Being bullied—How does it feel, and what can you do about it?	Activity sheet: "Being Bullied"
Reflecting on Key Messages	
Journal	Journal, writing materials

Introducing Key Messages

Literature

Choose and read a text that provides an example of how bullying can make a person feel.

Explain that bullying hurts everyone involved. Students who see or know bullying is happening may feel sad and worried about the situation. Most students dislike seeing other students being bullied. Students who often bully others are usually not very happy about themselves and may have trouble making and keeping friends. Similarly, students who are bullied often:

- Feel scared, alone, and sad
- Don't like coming to school
- Don't feel good about themselves
- Can feel sick and get headaches and stomachaches

Example Using *King of the Playground* by Phyllis Reynolds Naylor (1994)

Sammy is the king of the playground, and he won't let Kevin play on any of the equipment. He comes up with new crazy threats every day. When Kevin's dad suggests he use his own imagination to combat Sammy's bullying behavior, the two boys start a game and become friends.

Section 2

Activity—Graffiti

Arrange students into small groups, and discuss the characteristics of the following types of bullying situations. For example, how does it feel if you are bullied? What does it feel like if you are ignored or know that someone has spread a rumor about you that is not true?

Situations

- **Exclusion:**
  Someone is ignored, left out on purpose, or not allowed to join in.

- **Hurtful teasing and verbal abuse:**
  Someone is being made fun of and teased in a mean and hurtful way.

- **Rumors and lies:**
  Lies or nasty stories are being told about someone to make other students not like him or her.

- **Threats:**
  Someone is being made afraid of getting hurt.
  Someone is being stared at or given mean looks or gestures.
  Someone is being forced to do things he or she doesn't want to.

- **Physical bullying:**
  Someone is being hit, kicked, or pushed around.

- **Cyberbullying:**
  Hurtful messages or pictures are deliberately sent by mobile phone or using the Internet (email, social networking sites).

In groups of four, students write on a large sheet of paper words or phrases that they would use to describe what they would do to help someone in this situation. Discuss all groups' recommended actions.

Developing Key Messages

Literature

Read the story on the "New Boy" resource sheet to students, and discuss the reasons for the bullying behavior. Discuss the following questions.

- Why does Jeremy find it hard to make friends?
- How do you think he was feeling on his first day at a new school?
- Why did Jeremy behave the way he did?
- Can you suggest other ways Jeremy might have tried to join in?
- How do you think each of the characters in the story felt about Jeremy's behavior?
- Describe how the way each of the characters felt affected the way they responded to Jeremy's behavior.

Activity—Being Bullied: How Does It Feel, and What Can You Do About It?

Arrange the class in small groups, and give each group a copy of the "Being Bullied" activity sheet. Invite students to use the two blank spaces provided to write scenarios based on any situations they have seen at school (remind them not to use people's names). One member of the group reads each situation, and all group members suggest actions they could take to help themselves or others in this situation. Suggestions offered may range from asking someone for help, playing with another group of friends, or asking the person engaging in the bullying behavior to stop.

Reflecting on Key Messages

Student Journal

Ask students to write a few sentences about how they would feel if they were bullied and what they would do to help themselves. Stress that they should always take safe actions.

Ask students to pretend that an imaginary friend is bullying another student. Have students write a letter to the person bullying (imaginary friend) pointing out his or her bullying behavior and why they don't like it and would like him or her to stop. Ask students to explain how they would like their imaginary friend to behave instead.

Teacher Reflection

How effectively were the key messages developed?

To what extent are your students now able to:

- Identify feelings others may experience as a result of being bullied?
- Describe the possible physical and mental effects of bullying behavior?
- Demonstrate actions they can take to discourage bullying behavior?

Section 2

Chapter 13

Social Decision Making

Social Information Processing

~ SATAN AS A BOY ~

Social decision-making skills help us consider the consequences of our actions for ourselves and others and make thoughtful, sensible decisions. This involves:

- Understanding how a social situation makes us feel
- Considering the different choices we have and the positive and negative consequences of each of these choices when making a decision
- Making positive choices while considering how these choices may affect ourselves and others

Key Area 5: Social Decision Making

Focus	This Focus Will Enable Students to:	Focus Activities
1. Choices and consequences	• Demonstrate the use of a choices and consequences model to select appropriate actions to take to respond to bullying situations	• Discussion—What will I do? • Choices and consequences • Journal
2. Responding safely to bullying situations	• Identify when it is safe to respond to a bullying situation • Describe strategies they can use to respond in a safe way to a bullying situation • Plan strategies to effectively respond to bullying situations • Demonstrate actions to take to reduce harm caused by bullying	• Mind map • Situation cards • Action plan card pack • Take-home activity • Journal

Key Area 5: Social Decision Making

Social Information Processing

Focus 1: Choices and Consequences

Key Messages

Before deciding how to respond to a bullying situation we need to consider the consequences of the different choices we can make for ourselves and others.

This focus will enable students to:

- Demonstrate the use of a choices and consequences model to select appropriate actions to take to respond to bullying situations

Focus 1 Activities	Resources Needed
Introducing Key Messages	
Discussion—What will I do?	Chart paper
Developing Key Messages	
Choices and consequences	Activity sheet: "Choices and Consequences A" Resource sheet: "Choices and Consequences B"
Reflecting on Key Messages	
Journal	Journal, writing materials

Section 2

Introducing Key Messages

Discussion—What Will I Do?

Discuss what students need to consider when they are being bullied or see a bullying situation happening. For example:

- How does the bullying make you feel?
- What action needs to be taken?
- Is this action safe?
- Is this action fair to all involved?
- How will it make others feel?
- Does it solve the problem without creating more problems?

Create a chart with the words *think, plan, talk, do.* Explain to students that at the "Do: What am I going to do?" step, it is time to choose which action would be suitable and safe for the problem you are trying to sort out. There are often different actions you could choose for each situation, and it is sometimes difficult to decide which action is the best to take. One way of choosing the best action is to consider the consequences of each action. The consequences can be explained as: What good or not-so-good things might happen if I make this choice?

Developing Key Messages

Activity—Choices and Consequences

Introduce the pictorial decision-making model on the "Choices and Consequences A" activity sheet and work through the model with students. Arrange students in groups and give each group a copy of the "Choices and Consequences B" resource sheet. Read the situation, and ask each group to provide three possible actions it could take, and then discuss the positive and negative consequences of each action. As a class, discuss each group's choices, consequences, and decisions.

Reflecting on Key Messages

Student Journal

Ask students to interview at least one member of their family to find out any positive or negative consequences their family member experienced when he or she, or another person, tried to help someone who was being bullied. Encourage students to write a set of positive tips to themselves in their journal about what they can do to help someone without getting hurt themselves.

Teacher Reflection

How effectively were the key messages developed?

To what extent are your students now able to:

- Demonstrate the use of a choices and consequences model to select appropriate actions to take to respond to bullying situations?

Section 2

Focus 2: Responding Safely to Bullying Situations

Key Messages

Before responding to bullying situations, we need to make sure that it is safe to do so.

If the situation is not safe, we should always ask for help.

We need to know who to ask for help and where to find him or her.

This focus will enable students to:

- Identify when it is safe to respond to a bullying situation
- Describe strategies they can use to respond in a safe way to a bullying situation
- Plan strategies to effectively respond to bullying situations
- Demonstrate actions to take to reduce harm caused by bullying

Focus 2 Activities	Resources Needed
Introducing Key Messages	
Mind map	Writing and drawing materials
Developing Key Messages	
Situation cards	Resource sheets: "Situation Cards A and B"
Action plan card pack	Pack of blank index cards per child, writing materials, hole punch, and string or ribbon
Take-home activity	Activity sheet: "A Family Story"
Reflecting on Key Messages	
Journal	Journal, writing materials

Introducing Key Messages

Many people are not sure what to do if they or others are being bullied. There isn't one correct way to respond—it depends on the specific bullying situation. Explain to students there are some general strategies that work better than others, including asking themselves the following questions.

- *Can I handle this situation myself?* Explain to students that sometimes they may be involved in or see a situation that is too difficult or too dangerous to handle themselves, such as a fight between older students or someone bigger than you wanting to fight you. Discuss other examples and the reasons students should consider whether they can respond safely to the situation.
- *Do I need to ask for help?* Explain that if the situation is something students don't think they can handle or should get involved in, they can still take some action by asking for help. Discuss the importance of choosing people you can trust to go to for help and knowing where to find them.
- *What strategies could I use?* Ask students to consider ways to respond to a person who bullies. Discuss the benefits of being aware of a number of different strategies to respond to different types of bullying. For example, being called a mean name may require a different response than being hit.

Activity—Mind Map

Mind Maps for Kids: An Introduction by Tony Buzan (2003) is an excellent resource for familiarizing yourself and your students with mind maps, how to create them, and how to use them.

Ask students to mind map possible strategies for responding to bullying incidents.

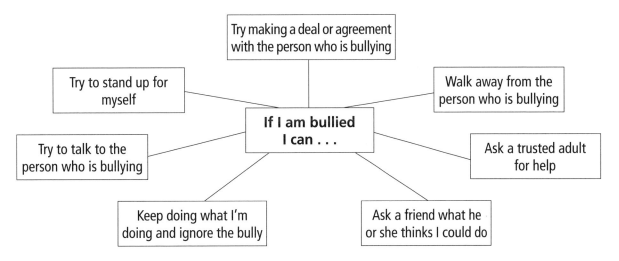

Figure 4: Mind map for responding to bullying incidents.

Developing Key Messages

Activity—Situation Cards

Arrange the class in groups of three, and give each group a set of situation cards prepared from the "Situation Cards A and B" resource sheets. Students place cards with the writing side facing down. Take turns to choose and read out a personal A or bystander B situation card. The students in each group discuss how it would make them feel if they were bullied or if they saw someone else being bullied in this way, and then the group plans suitable actions in response. Record all responses on a large piece of paper. Discuss with students that sometimes the actions we choose don't always get the response we might hope for. If the bullying continues, then we should think and plan again. These situation cards would also be suitable to laminate and hold together with a key ring.

Activity—Action Plan Card Pack

Using the actions and strategies compiled in the situation cards activity, give each student a set of blank index cards. Ask students to think about which strategies might work for them in different bullying situations—online or offline. Students record these on their blank cards. Cards can be hole-punched and a string or ribbon used to hold them together. Students now have their own pocket-sized *Action Plan Card Pack* to remind them of some positive actions they can take to respond to bullying situations.

Activity—Take-Home Activity

At the completion of the lesson, give each student a copy of the "A Family Story" activity sheet to take home and discuss with his or her family.

Reflecting on Key Messages

Student Journal

Students divide a page in their journal into three equal sections (see the following example). In each section, they write and respond to the question.

If I am being teased at school, I can . . .
If my friend is being deliberately left out, I can . . .
If my friend is bullying others, I could suggest . . .

Teacher Reflection

How effectively were the key messages developed?

To what extent are your students now able to:

- Identify when it is safe to respond to a bullying situation?
- Describe strategies they can use to respond in a safe way to a bullying situation?
- Plan strategies to effectively respond to bullying situations?
- Demonstrate actions to take to reduce harm caused by bullying?

Section 2

Teaching and Learning Resources

Middle Childhood

Teacher Resource
Ages 9–10

Self-Awareness

Sense of Self, Emotional Awareness

Self-awareness skills help us to recognize and understand our feelings while valuing our strengths and abilities. This involves:

- Being able to identify what we are feeling
- Understanding why we might feel a certain way
- Recognizing and having confidence to use our strengths and abilities

Key Area 1: Self-Awareness

Focus	This Focus Will Enable Students to:	Focus Activities
1. Exploring my values	• Identify values that are meaningful to them • Describe the importance of applying their values beyond the classroom to the wider community • Demonstrate putting their values into practice in social situations	• What do I value? • What have generations before me valued? • Literature • Mind map • My Valuables Box • Situation Shuffle—Values • Discussion—Values online • Promoting the message—Values quilt • Journal
2. Values and manners online and offline	• Identify manners and the role manners play in their lives • Describe common manners expected by the society in which they live • Demonstrate appropriate manners in all situations	• Literature • Manners Fest • Fork or Fingers? • Etiquette and netiquette • Manners • Journal
3. Values and social rules	• Identify social rules • Explain the reasons these rules exist • Demonstrate how to use social rules in different situations	• Snakes and Ladders • Kids' rules • Board game • Journal
4. Values in my community	• Identify values related to being part of their community • Describe the characteristics of a community whose members value each other's differences • Demonstrate ways they can help others in their community	• Community service • Journal

Key Area 1: Self-Awareness

Sense of Self, Emotional Awareness

Focus 1: Exploring My Values

Key Messages

Being aware of our own personal values and acting on these values help us feel good about ourselves.

Acting according to our values can sometimes be difficult.

We need to value people for who they are on the inside, not for what we can see on the outside, such as the clothes they wear, the house they live in, or the job they have.

This focus will enable students to:

- Identify values that are meaningful to them
- Describe the importance of applying their values beyond the classroom to the wider community
- Demonstrate putting their values into practice in social situations

Focus 1 Activities	Resources Needed
Introducing Key Messages	
What do I value?	Large sheets of paper
What have generations before me valued?	Writing materials
Developing Key Messages	
Literature	A text that provides an example of personal values (Sample text: *Storm Boy* by Colin Thiele, 2004)
Mind map	Large piece of paper
My Valuables Box	Container of each student's choice and decoration materials
Situation Shuffle—Values	Resource sheet: "Situation Shuffle: Values"
Discussion—Values online	
Promoting the message—Values quilt	See activity for materials.
Reflecting on Key Messages	
Journal	Journal, writing materials

Introducing Key Messages

Explain that a value is something we believe is important and worthwhile. Our values are defined by our attitudes, beliefs, and feelings. From a very early age, our values are influenced by our parents and family.

We value some areas of our life more than others, and what we value changes over time. Ask the students to recall something that was important to them when they were younger that is no longer as important. Record the students' answers. Once you know what is important to you, you are better equipped to stand up for yourself and make your own decisions about what you want to do. Another way of saying, "What's important to me" is to say, "I value . . . ," or "One of my values is . . ."

Explain that each person has different values and it is OK to be different. Some common values are related to:

- Physical appearance—Health, personal appearance
- Social acceptance—Friendship, family, respect, generosity, trust, love, fairness
- Athletic ability—Sports, fitness, physical strength, commitment, determination
- Academic ability—School, knowledge, learning, career
- Behavior—Responsibility, confidence, courtesy, kindness

Generate a class discussion centered on what is important to students and how they can best gather this information.

- Are there other categories you would like to include in the things you value? (For example, Internet use or being able to join social networking sites)
- Who and what influences the way you feel about certain things, and how important are they to you?
- What outside factors influence your values? (For example, books, the Internet, or TV shows and personalities)
- List three things you value most at this time in your life.

Activity—What Do I Value?

Arrange the students into small groups, and nominate one person to record responses. Ask the students to think about and discuss why knowing their own values is important. Each group records the most important reasons and provides feedback to the whole class. Collate a class list, and add any reasons that might be missing.

For example:

Knowing your values will help you to—

- Make decisions about what you want to do in life
- Choose goals that are right for you
- Take responsibility for yourself
- Stand up for yourself
- Understand and accept other people's values

Being very clear about what you value can be useful when you have difficult decisions to make.

- What can happen if you make a decision that goes against your values? For example, you are in a group, and students are teasing someone about the way he looks. While your friends are important to you, you also value treating other people fairly.

- How would you feel if you joined in with the teasing? How would you feel about yourself if you said nothing and just watched?

Discuss responses with the students.

If you would feel guilty, this is because kindness and acceptance of people's differences is a strong value of yours. Peer influence can be strong too, and friendships are important. This can make it difficult to avoid just going along with the group. What if you made the decision to stand by your values and stick up for the person being teased? The other students might tease you or get angry with you, but you will know you did what is right for you. Happiness and self-esteem come from making decisions and acting in a way that is true to your values, even when it is difficult.

Activity—What Have Generations Before Me Valued?

Our values change as we grow older and begin to feel differently about people and situations. Ask the students to interview and record the responses of three people from different generations about changes in their values from childhood to adulthood.

Some sample questions students may like to ask are:

- Thinking back to when you were as young as me, please tell me about one thing you owned that was more important to you than anything else.
- Do you still have it? Why do or did you value this so much?
- What was most important to you about weekends and school vacations?
- Can you name one value that has been a constant throughout your life?

The students share their findings. This could form the basis of a larger project in which the students create a comparison analysis for display in the classroom. The activity could also be extended to include values across different cultures.

Section 3

Developing Key Messages

Literature

Teacher note: The following story is a suggestion only, and teachers are encouraged to substitute a title of their choice if they wish.

Example Using *Storm Boy* by Colin Thiele (2004)

Storm Boy is an Australian classic. It contains strong messages relating to topics such as race relations, the environment, family structures, separation issues, and respect for people, animals, and the environment. Reading the book (and watching the DVD if available) with your students will provide opportunities to explore values on a number of levels. For example, the limitless capacity of the character Mr. Percival to expand his pouch can be likened to students' limitless capacity to expand their own social and emotional development through identification and exploration of their own set of personal values.

Some suggested activities and discussion points relating to *Storm Boy* include:

- Creating a mind map
- Identifying the characters and their values using a web
- Discussing how perceptions about other people can sometimes be incorrect
- Debating whether we have the right to judge how other people live

Activity—Mind Map

Mind Maps for Kids: An Introduction by Tony Buzan (2003) is an excellent resource for familiarizing yourself and your students with mind maps, how to create them, and how to use them.

The purpose of a mind map is to help the students organize their thoughts on a particular subject. Discuss with the students that it is an individual process—no two mind maps on the same subject ever look the same. This is because people don't think the same way or organize their thoughts in the same way.

Ask the students to design their own mind maps with the main topic in the center of the page being "I value . . ."

Activity—My Valuables Box

Ask the students to bring in or construct and decorate a box, bag, or something of their choice to be left in the classroom all year. They can place items they value into their box. Each student's box will contain different items and information. Ask the students what they think is meant by the expression *one person's trash is another person's treasure.* Use this expression to discuss with students that everyone has different values, and everyone has a right to have his or her values respected. During the year, the contents of the students' boxes may change, depending on the situations and events that occur in each student's life. Teachers may need to put constraints on box size, so the exercise is manageable within the classroom.

Activity—Situation Shuffle: Values

In groups of four, the students receive a set of cards from the "Situation Shuffle: Values" resource sheet. Copy, cut, and laminate the cards for future use.

The students shuffle the cards and spread them face down in the center of the group. Students take turns to choose a situation card and read it aloud for the group. Students answer the questions on the card and provide reasons for their responses. The students will develop an understanding that the "How would you feel?" question is important, because the strength of the feeling will indicate how important this issue is to them. If the feeling is not very strong, then this is likely to not be an important issue for them.

Each group can provide feedback to the class.

- What issues did students feel more strongly about than others?
- For what reasons did students feel more or less strongly about each issue?

Discussion—Values Online

Talking to people online can be quite different than talking to people face-to-face; as a result, we may not honor our values as we would face-to-face.

- What kinds of values, like being honest, might change when someone is communicating with another person online versus face-to-face?
- Can you describe a situation when someone might demonstrate a different set of values face-to-face and online, even though the situation is the same? For example, a student in your class is made fun of because she is not very good at sports.
  - If you see this happening on the playground, how would you react?
  - If you see this happening online, would you react the same or differently?
    ○ If so, how?
    ○ If not, can you explain why not?

Activity—Promoting the Message: Values Quilt

Have the students design a values quilt that represents things that are important to them at this point in their life. Fold an 8.5 x 11-inch piece of paper into four quadrants. Attach the finished sheets to a piece of fabric for presentation at an assembly. Alternatively, the values quilt could be created with muslin and stitched onto fabric. This longer-term project could involve the help of parents or guardians.

Section 3

Reflecting on Key Messages

Student Journal

Ask students to design a cover page for a reflection journal they will use throughout the year.

Discuss with students the benefits of keeping a journal. Explain that they will add to their journals throughout the year. This journal will encourage students to identify and record times when they live or witness others living their values. Allow flexibility in methods of recording; some students may prefer to write a report, others may prefer to compose a poem, and others may decide to express what they have witnessed in the form of artwork. Opportunities can be given for students to share journal entries with their classmates. If the students choose to share something about themselves, it should be stressed that this is not bragging about a good deed but rather displaying the ability to be able to make decisions about what you do in life based on the development of your own set of personal values.

Ask students to write answers to the following questions in their journals.

- Why should I respect other people's values?
- How can I do this?
- How can I be consistent with the way I treat other people?
- How easy is it for me to live my values?
- What makes it challenging for me to do this?
- How can I make sure I demonstrate the same set of values when interacting with other people offline and online?

Teacher Reflection

How effectively were the key messages developed?

To what extent are your students now able to:

- Identify values which are meaningful to them?
- Describe the importance of applying their values beyond the classroom to the wider community?
- Demonstrate putting their values into practice in social situations?

Focus 2: Values and Manners Online and Offline

Key Messages

Understanding why and how to use manners helps us know how to act in social situations. We should be accepting of all cultural differences, particularly those related to how to act in social situations.

This focus will enable students to:

- Identify manners and the role manners play in their lives
- Describe common manners expected by the society in which they live
- Demonstrate appropriate manners in all situations

Focus 2 Activities	Resources Needed
Introducing Key Messages	
Literature	A text that provides an example of using manners in a social situation
	(Sample texts: *Mind Your Manners, B. B. Wolf* by Judy Sierra, 2007, or *My Mouth Is a Volcano!* by Julia Cook, 2006)
Developing Key Messages	
Manners Fest	Large sheet of paper
Fork or Fingers?	Access to people from other cultures or access to the Internet
Etiquette and netiquette	
Manners	Activity sheet: "Manners"
Reflecting on Key Messages	
Journal	Journal, writing materials

Introducing Key Messages

Manners are valued by most cultures throughout the world. Discuss with the students that manners are polite behaviors and that polite words should be accompanied by polite actions, such as saying "thank you" with a smile and making eye contact with the person to whom you are speaking. Polite behavior is a sign of respect for other people. We are not born with a personal set of manners and values—they are learned from our social environment, such as parents, friends, and teachers. Acquiring manners as part of our values is a gradual process that occurs as we grow and develop. Having manners and using them in all sorts of situations help to give us confidence.

Most societies circulate certain values deemed important in allowing people to live together in a peaceful and cooperative environment.

Ask students to brainstorm a list of values that would be important to a community in which everyone gets along with each other, for example, peace, honesty, kindness, and so on. Ask the students to discuss why these values are important to a community.

Discuss with the students the impact of cultural differences in a multicultural society. For example, some cultures have different nose-blowing etiquette. Manners and the simple lessons of respect, which we learn as children, apply equally to all people.

- Why do people care about manners?
- How do you feel when you and another student get to the door at the same time, and the other student steps back and lets you go through first?
- How do you feel when a sibling snatches the last ice cream sandwich from your hand as you are getting it out of the freezer?

Literature

Choose and read a text that provides an example of using manners in a social situation. Conduct a guided discussion to identify the need for using manners in social situations. Use the events in the text to begin compiling a list of manners that are used and expected in our society. The chart can be added to and used as a reflection throughout the year.

Example Using *Mind Your Manners, B.B. Wolf* by Judy Sierra (2007)

The big bad wolf is trying to convince the three little pigs and the gingerbread man that he has changed. He does it all through song.

After reading the story, invite the students to write their own songs to tunes of their choice about specific manners and present these to the rest of the school at an assembly. This activity would be suitable as an individual or group activity. The messages in this story go deeper than the need for manners and provide opportunities for teachers to discuss with their students the importance of reciprocal friendships and respecting others.

Follow-up questions:

- How would you feel if you received an invitation to go to lunch with a special and important person?
- Would you feel nervous about knowing how to behave? Explain.
- If you were the crocodile, what advice would you have given the big bad wolf?

Other suitable titles:

My Mouth Is a Volcano! **by Julia Cook (2006)**

This book focuses on the very important life skill of not interrupting while other people are speaking. The story is told in such a way that students are provided with the opportunity to be able to join in the repeated verse throughout the story. The story also encourages students to look at a situation from other people's perspectives. The dramatization of this story could very easily be adapted to be performed at a school assembly. Older students could demonstrate to younger students that it is bad manners to interrupt while another person is speaking.

Follow-up questions:

- How would you feel if you were one of the people Louis is constantly interrupting?
- What would you say to Louis to help him stop interrupting?

Developing Key Messages

Activity—Manners Fest

In groups, ask the students to brainstorm examples of polite behaviors (both online and offline). For example, saying "thank you" or "sorry." Share the results with the class, and identify the most common good manners identified by students. These could be written on a large piece of paper and displayed in the classroom. Try sharing results in ways other than simply reporting. For example, a group may decide to mime polite behaviors. Other groups can take turns to guess which behavior they are miming. Another group might choose to present a rap song. Discuss the following.

- Do the simple manners we learned in kindergarten still apply in fourth grade?
- How would the world be different if people genuinely practiced their manners?
- How do we need to use manners when we are communicating online? What is meant by netiquette?

Section 3

Activity—Forks or Fingers?

As homework, ask the students to talk with someone from another culture about manners in their home and how they differ from those of the student's own home. Students may also choose to research this topic on the Internet and compile a comparison list of manners across different cultures.

- Is eating with your fingers good manners? It is if you live in some cultures!
- Do all cultures cover their mouths when they burp?

For example, in American culture, it is usually rude to be part of a group and not speak loud enough so that everyone can hear you. In Australian culture, it is usually considered bad manners if you talk loudly in a group situation to another person. It is seen as disturbing the rest of the group. The Forks or Fingers? activity could also form the basis of an assembly item, where students present skits on values in other cultures. Encourage them to draw on knowledge gained from their own families and friends who have roots in other cultures. Consider inviting someone from another culture to come and talk to the class about the different manners and values that exist in their culture. Encourage the speaker to discuss the difficulties this can cause when you move from one culture to another and how hard it can be to embrace a new culture while still holding onto the values from your home culture.

Activity—Etiquette and Netiquette

Etiquette and good manners are connected. Etiquette is not only about using good manners ourselves but also about making sure other people feel comfortable about the way we behave around them face-to-face. If everyone is familiar with the rules, this makes for more pleasant interactions in social situations.

Netiquette is a term derived from the combination of two words—*Internet* and *etiquette*. Netiquette refers to a set of rules for appropriate behavior to use when interacting in online environments including chat rooms, email, blogs, forums, and social networking sites.

Explain the rules of thumbs up, thumbs down, and thumbs away to the students. Thumbs up means you agree with the statement read by the teacher, thumbs down means you disagree, and thumbs away (sideways swipe) means you are not sure. The following statements are suggestions only, and teachers are invited to include statements of their own relating to netiquette.

In an online environment, you should:

- Only talk to people who you also know personally offline
- Not send or post a nasty message to anyone
- Remember there is always a real person with real feelings behind online avatars and usernames
- Make sure your messages are clear, as they can be misinterpreted
- Be aware people can't always tell the emotional tone of a written message
- Use smiley faces and emoticons to show if you are being silly or joking
- Never send a message when you are feeling angry; calm down and think about it clearly first
- Never send personal information about yourself or anyone else
- Remember that capital letters signify anger or yelling
- Ask for permission before taking or sending photos of other people online

Activity—Manners

Copy, cut, and laminate the "Manners" activity sheet. In pairs, ask the students to discuss what they should not do in each situation; if necessary, offer them suggestions. For example, someone that you already know is not nice offers you some food to eat. What don't you do? What can you try?

Reflecting on Key Messages

Student Journal

Ask students to list examples of manners they use at home, at school, and in the community. Provide an opportunity for students to share and explain the reason for using manners in these situations.

Teacher Reflection

How effectively were the key messages developed?

To what extent are your students now able to:

- Identify manners and the role manners play in their lives?
- Describe common manners expected by the society in which they live?
- Demonstrate appropriate manners in all situations?

Focus 3: Values and Social Rules

Key Messages

Using manners shows we care about and respect others.

Social rules within cultures are used by people with good manners.

This focus will enable students to:

- Identify social rules
- Explain the reasons these rules exist
- Demonstrate how to use social rules in different situations

Focus 3 Activities	Resources Needed
Introducing Key Messages	
Snakes and Ladders	Resource sheet: "Snakes and Ladders"
Developing Key Messages	
Kids' rules	Paper, colored pens
Board game	See activity for materials.
Reflecting on Key Messages	
Journal	Journal, writing materials

Introducing Key Messages

In order to function in an organized way, communities establish rules that all members are expected to follow. Some rules (often described as written) are easy to recognize, because they are clearly stated and often visibly displayed. For example, a stop sign is recognized by everyone as a place cars should stop to check for traffic, or a no entry sign signifies when a road is closed.

The *unwritten* rules are sometimes a little harder to understand, but they are also expected to be followed, so that communities can function in a peaceful and respectful manner. An example of an unwritten rule is the expectation that people will say "please" when they want something and "thank you" when they are given something. Different cultures have their own set of written and unwritten rules that reflect the values of that culture.

- Have you met anyone from another culture and had difficulty understanding some of the rules that they follow?
- List some examples.

Rules are necessary to make sure organizations such as schools run smoothly and also to keep people safe. Written and unwritten rules help our friendship groups function in cooperative ways. Trying to understand the unwritten rules of friendship can sometimes be the cause of conflict among friends. Discuss with students the written and unwritten rules of the groups they are part of, including family groups. The following are some suggested questions to begin the discussion.

- What are some of the written and unwritten rules in your family?
- How do these rules help your family get along better?
- How are the unwritten rules influenced by your own and your family's values? For example, your family members may like their home to be very neat and tidy and there is a strong (unwritten) rule that you will keep your room and other areas of your home tidy.

After discussing these questions, students form groups and use the questions to examine rules, both written and unwritten, within the classroom, school playground, community, and online, for example, when using social networking sites or instant messaging, when part of a local sporting team, at the local swimming pool, or in a church group.

Teacher note: *The Unwritten Rules of Friendship* by Natalie Madorsky Elman and Eileen Kennedy-Moore (2003) is an excellent resource for parents and teachers. Each chapter focuses on the different personality traits of children (for example, the shy child, the short-fused child, or the different drummer) and suggests how to support these children in their journey toward more positive peer relationships. Some chapters include innovative game ideas aimed at developing positive prosocial skills.

Section 3

Activity—Snakes and Ladders

Place an enlarged copy of the "Snakes and Ladders" resource sheet on the board, and explain to students that you (as the teacher) are going to challenge the class in a game to see who gets to the end first. During the game, don't follow the rules. For example, when you don't get the number you want, you throw the dice again, jump over snakes when you are supposed to land on them, climb up ladders even when you don't land on the squares, and so on. When students object to your behavior, ask them to explain to you why you can't do things the way you want. Some answers they may offer include:

- It is against the rules.
- It is unfair for the other players because everybody should have the same chance to play and win.
- There is no point in playing the game without rules.

Developing Key Messages

Activity—Kids' Rules

Ask the students to gather into small groups. Explain that they will be designing a set of school rules they think other students in the school need to follow. They need to assess the rules to make sure they fit the following criteria for a good rule.

- Will everyone understand what the rule means?
- Is the rule fair to everyone?
- Will everyone be able to follow the rule?
- Are rules about online behavior included as well as offline behavior?
- Does the rule describe positive behavior rather than negative? For example, instead of "Don't swear," say "Speak politely."
- Do we know what the consequence or penalty will be if the rule is not followed? Penalties should relate to the behavior in some way. For example, if a student leaves garbage behind he or she should clean up a certain area of the schoolyard.

Ask each group to present its set of rules to the class. A combined set of voted best rules could then be presented to the staff or principal as suggestions for implementation in the school. This activity would also be suitable for group presentation at a school assembly to promote the message that rules help our school function in a more harmonious way.

Activity—Board Game

Provide the students with materials they can use to make board games, such as dice, markers, blocks, cardboard, and felt-tip pens. Encourage the students to source materials from home. In groups of two or three, the students devise their own board game and create rules for playing the game. Ask each group to explain its completed game to the class and have a game session where students are able to test the games. The games could also be used to play with younger students and played during buddy sessions. Discuss with the class why rules are necessary to play the games created. What unwritten rules should we all follow when playing games (for example, being kind, sharing space, and helping others if they are having difficulty)?

Reflecting on Key Messages

Student Journal

Ask each student to think and write about the following points in his or her journal.

- Why is it important to be aware of and respect the rules—written and unwritten—affecting students from other cultures within our school?
- How do you feel when you visit a friend's home and the rules are a bit different from the rules in your own home? What do you do in these situations?

Teacher Reflection

How effectively were the key messages developed?

To what extent are your students now able to:

- Identify social rules?
- Explain the reasons these rules exist?
- Demonstrate how to use social rules in different situations?

Section 3

Focus 4: Values in My Community

Key Messages

Contributing to our community helps us appreciate the values associated with being a part of something larger than ourselves.

This focus will enable students to:

- Identify values related to being part of their community
- Describe the characteristics of a community whose members value each other's differences
- Demonstrate ways they can help others in their community

Focus 4 Activities	Resources Needed
Introducing Key Messages	
Community service	
Reflecting on Key Messages	
Journal	Journal, writing materials

Introducing Key Messages

Explain to the students that it is possible to go through life only looking out for yourself and thinking about what best suits you and how to achieve this. Discuss the importance of developing an awareness of the people in your community and considering the ways you can help them. Once you begin doing something for someone else without expecting something in return, you will be surprised how much you get back. "Getting back" can take many forms, for example, feeling good about yourself, establishing a new friendship, or learning a new skill.

Explain to the students how it feels to give your time, or something else important to you, to others. It is possible to donate money to worthy causes, and it is also important to do this, so that organizations can continue to do their jobs successfully. Giving your time requires more effort; however, the rewards make it worthwhile.

Encourage the students to consider who in their neighborhood they could offer to help. For example, an elderly person who would appreciate someone putting out and bringing in his or her garbage cans.

Remind the students that they need to enlist the help of their parents or guardians when investigating these possibilities to ensure their safety at all times. Ask the students to discuss with a partner and then report to the class what they see as some of the benefits of helping others in the community.

Following is a list of benefits you can draw to the students' attention if they are not included in their reports.

- Gaining a better understanding of what it means to be responsible and commit to helping others
- Learning to be tolerant of people in different situations
- Understanding the value of giving up your time or possessions to make a difference to another person
- Learning a new skill
- Finding new ways to spend your time
- Realizing that as individuals they *can* make a difference

Activity—Community Service

Collect information about recipients of community service awards, and share their stories with the class. Encourage the students to search local newspapers and magazines and watch the news to gather information about other people or groups' involvement in the local community. The students can also find information online with their teacher's or parent's help.

Ask students to invite someone they have researched locally who takes part in community projects to come and talk to the class about how he or she got started, why he or she wanted to be involved, and how he or she feels about his or her involvement. Help the students to source contact details.

Ask students to brainstorm ways they can find out about local community projects, which may be looking for input from students in fourth grade. Contacting the city council is a good starting point.

Reflecting on Key Messages

Student Journal

Ask students to reflect on and write short answers to the following questions.

- Can you remember a time when you have helped a neighbor, friend, or relative? In a few sentences, describe the situation.
- How did you feel?
- Why do you think it is important to develop a practice of helping others?

Teacher Reflection

How effectively were the key messages developed?

To what extent are your students now able to:

- Identify values related to being part of their community?
- Describe the characteristics of a community whose members value each other's differences?
- Demonstrate ways they can help others in their community?

Section 3

Chapter 15

Self-Management

Emotional Regulation, Resilience, and Self-Motivation

NORMAN HAD EXTRAORDINARY SOCIAL AWARENESS

HE CREDITED THIS TO AN EXPERIENCE IN HIS CHILDHOOD

WHICH INVOLVED BAKED BEANS AND AN EXPRESS LIFT

Self-management skills enable us to control and direct our emotions in appropriate ways. This involves:

- Managing our emotions so they don't stop us from effectively dealing with situations and pursuing our goals
- Striving to achieve our goals despite difficulties

Section 3

Key Area 2: Self-Management

Focus	This Focus Will Enable Students to:	Focus Activities
1. Resolving conflict	• Identify positive actions they can take to resolve conflicts • Describe the difference between win-win, win-lose, and lose-lose conflict resolution • Demonstrate strategies to use in win-win conflict resolution	• Just suppose • Think about • Discussion • Lose-lose, win-lose, win-win • Journal
2. When it's OK to say "no"	• Identify the types of situations when it's OK to say "no" • Predict the effect on themselves and others of saying "no" in social situations • Demonstrate saying "no" confidently in role-play situations	• When it's OK to say "no" • Saying "no" in the real world • Journal
3. Standing up for what you believe in and value	• Identify situations that challenge what they believe in and value • Describe how the decisions they make can be influenced by their values • Predict ways to maintain positive control of their emotions in challenging situations • Demonstrate positive responses that reflect their personal values in response to conflict situations	• Literature • Think, pair, share • Journal

Key Area 2: Self-Management

Emotional Regulation, Resilience, and Self-Motivation

Focus 1: Resolving Conflict

Key Messages

There are actions that can be taken to resolve conflict positively.

Always try to work toward a win-win outcome when resolving conflict.

This focus will enable students to:

- Identify positive actions they can take to resolve conflicts
- Describe the difference between win-win, win-lose, and lose-lose conflict resolution
- Demonstrate strategies to use in win-win conflict resolution

Focus 1 Activities	Resources Needed
Introducing Key Messages	
Just suppose	List of conflict situations compiled by students, spinner
Think about	
Developing Key Messages	
Discussion	Resource sheet: "Sorting Out a Conflict"
Lose-lose, win-lose, win-win	Resource sheet: "Conflict Situations"
Reflecting on Key Messages	
Journal	Journal, writing materials

Section 3

Introducing Key Messages

Explain to students that everyone will be involved in conflict situations at different times in his or her life. How we respond will in part determine whether the outcomes experienced are positive or negative. Typically, when two people fight, they both want to win, which usually means that one wins and one loses. If people have positive strategies to resolve conflict, the result may be that while neither party gets exactly what he or she wanted, he or she may be able to reach an agreement and importantly remain friends. Conflict resolution encourages those involved to work out ways to deal positively with the conflict. Discuss with students the benefit to themselves and others of learning how to resolve their own conflicts rather than relying on others to solve conflicts for them. Stress to students that if they do not feel safe in any conflict, they should always ask a trusted adult for help.

Ask the students to get into groups and brainstorm a list of common causes of conflict at school, home, or in the community and display the results. Some examples may include:

- There is only one piece of cake left, and you and your brother or sister both want it.
- Your best friend always wants to choose what game you both play.
- There is only one computer at home, and you feel you don't get as much time on it as everyone else in the family.
- You go to the local skate park every Saturday and use a particular section of the ramp. Another person has started coming at the same time and using the area you always use.

Encourage the students to offer solutions to these potential conflict situations. Possible solutions may include, but not be limited to:

- One sibling cutting the piece of cake and the other choosing one piece
- Tossing a coin or taking turns deciding what to play
- Taking turns on the computer for an equal length of time, using a timer to make sure time is divided equally
- Offering to take turns using the ramp

Activity—Just Suppose

Use a spinner from a class board game, or design your own, to use as an alternative way of choosing students for activities. Ask the students to form a circle sitting on the floor. Place the spinner in the middle. Invite one student to spin. Ask the student seated where the spinner stops to choose one of the conflict situations brainstormed earlier to read to the rest of the class or to provide his or her own scenario. For example:

"Just suppose you and your sister go to the fridge to get an ice cream sandwich at the same time. There is only one left, and you both believe you are entitled to it."

What could you do? Students provide a list of possible solutions. Allow time for the discussion to include why some solutions might work better than others.

Activity—Think About

Explain to the students that not all conflict situations are easy to resolve. Discuss with the class what happens when two people firmly believe they are both right about something and refuse to back down. Explain that it can be difficult to solve any conflict when you are more focused on winning than finding a solution. Discuss with the students the importance of controlling your anger and using strategies to try and reach an outcome that is fair to all parties.

Discuss with the students the characteristics of a win-win, win-lose, or lose-lose outcome in a situation that involves conflict.

- **Win-win:** In this situation everyone feels happy with the outcome.
- **Win-lose:** In this situation some people are not happy with the outcome.
- **Lose-lose:** In this situation no one feels happy with the outcome.

Use the following example to demonstrate the three outcomes.

Two boys fight to be leader in the line. Each student believes he was first in line and wants to have the front position.

Lose-lose:

The students continue to fight, pushing and shoving and yelling. The teacher sends both students to the vice principal's office.

- What are the consequences of this situation?
- Is it fair to both parties? Explain your reasons.

Win-lose:

The students continue to fight for the position; however, the bigger of the two boys pushes the smaller boy over and takes the front position.

- What are the consequences of this situation?
- Is it fair to both parties? Explain your reasons.

Win-win:

The two boys realize they probably both got there at the same time and agree to play Rock-Paper-Scissors to see who goes first.

- What are the consequences of this situation?
- Is it fair to both parties? Explain your reasons.

Section 3

Developing Key Messages

Discussion

Discuss with the students some tips for resolving a conflict on the "Sorting Out a Conflict" resource sheet. Provide an enlarged photocopied version (laminated if possible) for students to refer to in the classroom. It can also be useful to display on the playground.

1. Treat each other with respect; no blaming or put-downs. Talk in quiet, calm voices.

2. Attack the problem, not the person. Think about the problem, and brainstorm solutions.

3. Wait for your turn to speak; no interrupting.

4. Repeat what you think was said to you (this is not agreeing with the other person; it is letting him or her know that you understand what he or she is saying and how he or she is feeling).

5. Work together to find a fair solution for both parties, and stick to what you have decided.

6. Present your view of the situation in a truthful way.

7. Talk again if the solution is not working, and then if you can't work it out, ask for help.

Follow-up questions:

- How many of the suggestions would still apply if the conflict was happening online? For example, how do you treat each other with respect and talk in quiet, calm voices online?
- What are some of the barriers (difficulties) to resolving conflicts occurring online?

Activity—Lose-Lose, Win-Lose, Win-Win

In groups of three, ask the students to select one conflict situation from the "Conflict Situations" resource sheet, which can be copied, cut, and laminated to be used again. Ask the group to discuss and record three options for resolving its conflict: lose-lose, win-lose, and win-win. Ask students to discuss and record the effects of each of these options on the people involved. Ask one representative from each group to share his or her ideas and to explain briefly the effects of each response on the people involved.

Reflecting on Key Messages

Student Journal

Ask the students to reflect and write about what they find hard to deal with when they are trying to resolve conflict with others. Ask the students to record one action they could take to help them achieve more positive outcomes in conflict resolution.

Teacher Reflection

How effectively were the key messages developed?

To what extent are your students now able to:

- Identify positive actions they can take to resolve conflicts?
- Describe the difference between win-win, win-lose, and lose-lose conflict resolution?
- Demonstrate strategies to use in win-win conflict resolution?

Section 3

Focus 2: When It's OK to Say "No"

Key Messages

It is OK to say "no" if you feel uncomfortable about something.

It is possible to say "no" to a friend and still remain friends.

This focus will enable students to:

- Identify the types of situations when it's OK to say "no"
- Predict the effect on themselves and others of saying "no" in social situations
- Demonstrate saying "no" confidently in role-play situations

Focus 2 Activities	Resources Needed
Introducing Key Messages	
When it's OK to say "no"	Resource sheet: "When It's OK to Say 'No'"
Developing Key Messages	
Saying "no" in the real world	
Reflecting on Key Messages	
Journal	Journal, writing materials

Introducing Key Messages

Explain to the students that if someone asks us to do something we believe is wrong or unsafe, we can say "no" or "no thanks" even though we might find it hard to do. Discuss why we don't have to provide a reason for saying "no." Sometimes how our body reacts to a request, and how we feel inside (that funny feeling in our tummy) will help us to decide if we want to participate or if we want to say "no thanks."

Explain to the students the importance of thinking carefully about the difference between comfortable and reasonable requests and uncomfortable requests. Explain to the students there might be times when we aren't sure about what we want to say or how we feel. Some useful lines to remember to allow time to think about what is being asked of us and decide if we want to participate include:

"I am not sure about this. Can I let you know tomorrow?"

"Can you give me a little more information, please?"

If we say "no" to a person, it does not mean we are rejecting him or her, but just rejecting what he or she has asked us to do. The body language we use can be powerful in these situations. Standing tall, looking the other person straight in the eye, and putting our hands on our hips can all be strong indicators to others that when we say "no" we really mean it. Ask students to suggest other body language they can use to send a polite "no" message to others.

Developing the confidence to say "no" helps develop our self-esteem. Taking time to consider the consequences of a request before responding and practicing various ways of saying "no" increase our capacity to make safe decisions under pressure. Requests that we know are wrong can come from many sources, not just from our friends and siblings. Uncomfortable requests can also come from people online (who we know and don't know) such as through a social networking site or instant messaging. Online requests can be even more difficult to manage as we cannot be 100 percent sure where the request is coming from. Ask the students to discuss what actions they can take to feel safe if they feel pressured by an unreasonable request online.

Reinforce to the students:

- If it does not feel right, then it probably isn't.
- If you don't know how to handle a situation, always ask for help from a trusted adult.

Activity—When It's OK to Say "No"

Copy, cut, laminate, and attach cards from the "When It's OK to Say 'No'" resource sheet to a three-ring binder. Provide one set for each group of three to four students. Cards describe three types of scenarios:

1. When refusal is not an option
2. When refusal is easy
3. When refusal is difficult

Two blank spaces are provided for students to create their own scenarios. Ask the members of each group to:

- Identify whether the situation on their card is easy, difficult, or not an option to respond with "no"
- Take turns practicing different ways of saying "no" to the requests on the cards, remembering to include body language in their responses
- Act out their responses to the rest of the class

Allocate time for the students to provide constructive feedback and offer alternative suggestions. Before students commence this activity, brainstorm some sentence starters they could use when faced with the task of refusal.

For example: "You are a friend, but . . ."

Section 3

Developing Key Messages

Activity—Saying "No" in the Real World

Ask the students to search for articles in newspapers and magazines in which thinking about consequences of actions and knowing how to say "no" might have resulted in a different outcome to what happened in the article. Example articles could be about road rage, road deaths caused by drunk drivers, violence between two or more people, or the death of a child after participating in risky behavior with friends. In a circle, read articles the students have selected, and ask them to suggest what actions could have been taken to enable a more positive outcome.

Reflecting on Key Messages

Student Journal

Ask the students to reflect on and answer the following.

- How easy or difficult do I find it to say "no" when others ask me to do something I am not comfortable doing?
- How can I say "no" more confidently, without risking losing my friends?
- Write about one thing a friend asked you to do that made you feel uncomfortable.
- What did you do in this situation, and what else could you have done?

Teacher Reflection

How effectively were the key messages developed?

To what extent are your students now able to:

- Identify the types of situations when it's OK to say "no"?
- Predict the effect on themselves and others of saying "no" in social situations?
- Demonstrate saying "no" confidently in role-play situations?

Focus 3: Standing Up for What You Believe in and Value

Key Messages

We all think differently, and our values influence how we respond to conflict.

Standing up for what you believe in and value helps you become more confident and boosts your self-esteem.

This focus will enable students to:

- Identify situations that challenge what they believe in and value
- Describe how the decisions they make can be influenced by their values
- Predict ways to maintain positive control of their emotions in challenging situations
- Demonstrate positive responses that reflect their personal values in response to conflict situations

Focus 3 Activities	Resources Needed
Introducing Key Messages	
Literature	A text that provides an example of standing up for what you believe in (Sample text: *The Recess Queen* by Alexis O'Neill, 2002)
Developing Key Messages	
Think, pair, share	Activity sheet: "Standing Up for Your Beliefs"
Reflecting on Key Messages	
Journal	Journal, writing materials

Section 3

Introducing Key Messages

Explain to the students that what we value is influenced from an early age by the beliefs taught to us by our parents and caregivers. This affects the way we feel and respond to situations, including conflict situations. As we get older, we will not always agree with others' beliefs and values. When this happens, it can be hard to respond in appropriate ways to situations in which we believe others are not being treated fairly.

Discuss the following questions with the students.

- What actions can you take to stand up for what you believe in without offending others and without putting yourself at risk?
- What factors might stop you from speaking out or acting on something you see happening on the playground? (Some answers might include students being scared or feeling they may be hurt or targeted next, not knowing what words to use, or not being sure of the reaction they will get.)
- How much of what you believe and value is influenced by people in your life who teach you the "right thing" to do?
- When can it be hard to know the right thing to do when you are online?
- Who can help you when you are online and are faced with situations that you believe are not OK?

Ask the students to share their stories on significant role models in their lives and the influence they have on how they care and show respect to others online and offline.

Literature

Read a text that provides an example of standing up for what you believe in. Conduct a guided discussion to identify the values and beliefs demonstrated in the text and how they influenced behavior.

Example Using *The Recess Queen* by Alexis O'Neill (2002)

This story is about Katie Sue who stands up for what she believes in. She thinks the way Mean Jean bosses the other students around and tells them what they can and can't do on the playground and hurts them is unfair. She wants to stand up to Mean Jean but she also wants to make sure she and the other students are safe, so she thinks of a clever way to make this happen.

Follow-up questions:

- Have you ever seen someone behaving like Mean Jean?
- How did you feel when you saw these behaviors?
- What other actions could Katie Sue take to show Mean Jean that she did not approve of the way she was treating other students?

Developing Key Messages

Activity—Think, Pair, Share

Arrange the students in pairs, and give each pair one of the situations from the "Standing Up for Your Beliefs" activity sheet. Ask students to first consider and then record what actions they might take in this situation. Ask the students to share their thoughts with their partner. Invite selected students to share their responses with the class.

Reflecting on Key Messages

Student Journal

Ask students to reflect on and write short answers to the following questions.

- How am I able to stand up for myself if I think someone is treating me unfairly?
- Do I stand up for others if I feel they are being treated unfairly?
- If not, what stops me from doing this?
- What other actions can I take to stand up for myself and others if I see them being treated unfairly?

Teacher Reflection

How effectively were the key messages developed?

To what extent are your students now able to:

- Identify situations that challenge what they believe in and value?
- Describe how the decisions they make can be influenced by their values?
- Predict ways to maintain positive control of their emotions in challenging situations?
- Demonstrate positive responses that reflect their personal values in response to conflict situations?

Section 3

Chapter 16

Social Awareness

Understanding and Interpreting Social Situations

Social awareness skills help us to be aware and respectful of the feelings and perspectives of others. This involves:

- Recognizing what others may be feeling
- Trying to understand a situation from another's point of view
- Accepting and valuing people who are different from ourselves

Key Area 3: Social Awareness

Focus	This Focus Will Enable Students to:	Focus Activities
1. Friends and friendship groups	• Identify reciprocal friends and friendship groups • Describe the influence of values on friendship and positive friendship groups • Demonstrate actions they can take to promote positive communication and cooperation in friendship groups	• Literature • A tale of two plants • Friendship firsts • Friendship toolkit • The friendship shuffle • Journal
2. Equality and exclusion in groups	• Identify fairness, equality, and exclusion in groups • Describe behaviors and attitudes that reflect treating people fairly and equally • Demonstrate fostering a culture of fairness and equality within our school community	• Literature • Y chart for equality and exclusion • Shape Town • Journal
3. Empathy— Understanding how others feel	• Identify times when they need to try to understand how others may be feeling • Predict how others may be feeling • Apply strategies to demonstrate their understanding of others' feelings	• Literature • Do you feel what they feel? • Feelings charades • Shoe shuffle • Journal

Key Area 3: Social Awareness

Understanding and Interpreting Social Situations

Focus 1: Friends and Friendship Groups

Key Messages

There are many actions we can take as a friend to build positive friendship groups.

Behaviors which start and help maintain positive friendships are known as *social skills*.

This focus will enable students to:

- Identify reciprocal friends and friendship groups
- Describe the influence of values on friendship and positive friendship groups
- Demonstrate actions they can take to promote positive communication and cooperation in friendship groups

Focus 1 Activities	Resources Needed
Introducing Key Messages	
Literature	A text that provides an example of respectful behavior between friends (Sample text: *Pearl Barley and Charlie Parsley* by Aaron Blabey, 2007)
Developing Key Messages	
A tale of two plants	Two plants
Friendship firsts	Resource sheet: "Friendship Firsts"
Friendship toolkit	Poster board, drawing materials
The Friendship Shuffle	Activity sheet: "The Friendship Shuffle"
Reflecting on Key Messages	
Journal	Journal, writing materials

Section 3

Introducing Key Messages

Friends are very important to us all. They spend time with us and support us. They usually have similar values and beliefs as us. One friend who is often overlooked is the one we have with us all the time, ourself. Knowing what friendship is helps us to know how to be a good friend.

Having friends online can be a little more complex, because we cannot always be sure that the people we are communicating with are exactly who they say they are. We only talk to people online when we know who they are and we trust them.

In groups, ask students to brainstorm words they associate with friends and friendship groups. Allow students the flexibility to present their findings to the class in a variety of ways. Suggest mind maps and Y charts to groups who are having difficulty deciding how to present their findings.

Generate a discussion with students about what friendship is, using the following starter questions.

- What qualities are important to you in a friend?
- Is friendship important to you? Explain why.
- Is there a difference between being a friend and having a friend? If yes, explain the differences.
- Do friends always have fun together?
- If you had an argument with a friend, how did it feel?
- What actions did you take to try to be friends again?
- Is face-to-face friendship the same as online friendship? If not, why not?
- What actions can you take to stay safe in an online environment?
- Name some good and not-so-good aspects of online friendships.
- What qualities are important to you in an online friend?

Being able to talk about problems as they arise with your friendship group, rather than letting them build up until they are out of control, is a good way to make sure that all members of the group understand what is going on and how they are affected. Ask students to think about how their friendship groups work by answering the following questions.

- What do you like best about the friendship groups to which you belong?
- How does it make you feel when your group is not getting along?
- Do members of your group respond in the same way to conflict situations? If not, explain the different behaviors.
- What makes your group work well?
- If you were to rate your group's cooperation level on a scale of 1–5 (1 being low, 5 being high) what would it be this week?
- Can you think of some ways your group could work toward being more cooperative?

Literature

Choose and read a text that provides an example of respectful behavior between friends. Conduct a guided discussion to create a list of behaviors that are important in establishing and maintaining friendships.

Example Using *Pearl Barley and Charlie Parsley* by Aaron Blabey (2007)

This picture book illustrates how friends do not need to be alike. It shows that the strength of their friendship lies in them being able to accept each other's differences and always treat each other with care and respect.

Follow-up questions:

- Pearl Barley and Charlie Parsley *complement* each other. What does this mean?
- Do you have a friend who you complement? Explain in what ways you do this.
- What is this story trying to tell us about friendship?

Other suitable titles:

"Promises, Promises," a short story in *Hot Issues, Cool Choices* by Sandra McLeod Humphrey (2007)

Developing Key Messages

Activity—A Tale of Two Plants

Provide two plants, and explain to the students they are going to conduct an experiment. Over a one-month period, ask the students (using a roster system) to take care of one of the plants by watering it, making sure it is in a position where it gets some sunlight, feeding it with some fertilizer, talking to it if they like, and watching it grow. Give the other plant no attention. At the end of the month, ask the students to compare the two plants.

- Which looks healthier and why?
- If we treated friends or friendship groups the same way we treated the plants, what predictions could you make?

Activity—Friendship Firsts

There are many actions you can take to make sure you are a good friend. In groups of four, ask the students to draw one card from the precut laminated cards on the "Friendship Firsts" resource sheet. Ask the students to discuss whether the information on the card would be useful to them when trying to make new friends. Ask each group to brainstorm at least two more positive actions students could take when making new friends, and share these with the class.

Section 3

Activity—Friendship Toolkit

Explain to students that friendships need to be maintained, just like other things you value, for example, your skateboard, baseball bat, or swimming pool. If they are not maintained, they don't work as well. Provide the students with a piece of poster board on which to design a friendship toolkit. Ask the students to decide what needs to be added to this toolkit to maintain friendships. The students can represent the various tools in any way they wish. Some may see that for friendships to flourish they need to be able to keep a promise, so they might include a small box with a key with the word *promises* written on the outside. Others may include a happy face, indicating that friends like to be surrounded by cheerful, happy people. Some may include a joke, representing the importance of having a sense of humor with your friends. Invite the students to share their individual toolkits with the class.

Activity—The Friendship Shuffle

Explain to the students that sometimes we want to make new friends but are not sure how to do this. Other times we want to say something to a friend in our group about his or her behavior but do not want to hurt his or her feelings or risk losing him or her as a friend. Discuss the value of practicing what to say in these situations. Arrange the students in small groups, and ask each group to select one of the precut cards from "The Friendship Shuffle" activity sheet. Ask the students to share and record responses to the situations. Invite the students to report on some of their most common responses to the other groups. Two blank boxes are provided for the students to supply their own situations.

Reflecting on Key Messages

Student Journal

Ask students to reflect on and write about actions they can take to be a better friend. Ask students to create and illustrate a poem titled "What Friendship Means to Me."

Teacher R eflection

How effectively were the key messages developed?

To what extent are your students now able to:

- Identify reciprocal friends and friendship groups?
- Describe the influence of values on friendship and positive friendship groups?
- Demonstrate actions they can take to promote positive communication and cooperation in friendship groups?

Focus 2: Equality and Exclusion in Groups

Key Messages

We have a right to be treated fairly and to be included in friendship groups.

We have a responsibility to treat others fairly and to not exclude them from friendship groups.

The focus will enable students to:

- Identify fairness, equality, and exclusion in groups
- Describe behaviors and attitudes that reflect treating people fairly and equally
- Demonstrate fostering a culture of fairness and equality within our school community

Focus 2 Activities	Resources Needed
Introducing Key Messages	
Literature	A text that provides an example of exclusive and inclusive behaviors in a social situation (Sample text: *Clancy the Courageous Cow* by Lachie Hume, 2007)
Y chart for equality and exclusion	Paper, writing materials
Developing Key Messages	
Shape Town	Resource sheet: "Shape Town" Resource sheet: "Shapes From Shape Town" Resource sheet: "A Rainy Day in Shape Town" Resource sheet: "Template for Shape Wall"
Reflecting on Key Messages	
Journal	Journal, writing material

Section 3

Introducing Key Messages

Explain to the students that we all deserve to be respected and treated fairly and equally. When we respect and treat others fairly, we do not judge them because they sound or look different, are a different gender, culture, or race, or have different beliefs. We see each person as unique and special. Explain to students that this means we do not accept poor social behavior (treating other people badly), including bullying. Explain that exclusion is when someone is left out or barred from joining in, sometimes deliberately. Discuss with students the following examples, and ask students to provide examples of their own.

- Being left out of the group at recess time
- Not being chosen for a group activity
- Not being allowed to play with your friends
- Being told to get lost
- Being left out or removed from a friend's online social networking list or defriended

Discuss with the students how including others in activities and games helps everyone feel accepted and good about him- or herself. Including others implies we are generous and prepared to share some of our time and ideas with others. It makes others feel we are interested in them and care about their feelings. Including others in our games will make them feel like doing the same for us. Ask the students what they think is meant by the saying: "You get back what you give out."

Ask the students to discuss in small groups and report their opinions on the following questions back to the class.

- How can it be easy to exclude others online? What can you do to be sure that friends online don't feel left out, such as when you are instant messaging or playing an online game?
- How is being treated with respect or being excluded different or similar when you are online with your friends compared to being with them face-to-face?

Literature

Choose and read a text that provides an example of exclusive and inclusive behaviors in a social situation. Conduct a guided discussion to identify and list the behaviors and the impact they had on the characters in the text. Encourage students to add additional inclusive behaviors to the list.

Example Using *Clancy the Courageous Cow* by Lachie Hume (2007)

Clancy is a Belted Galloway, a black cow with a white stripe, but he has been born without a stripe, and because of this he is excluded from the rest of the herd. No matter what he tries to do to fit in, it doesn't work, and Clancy realizes that he will always be different. What this story celebrates is that it is OK to be different and that with a little courage and determination we can all find a place where we feel comfortable.

Follow-up questions:

- How do you think Clancy felt when the other cows made fun of him? Why did Clancy try so many ways to become like the other cows?

- Did being loved dearly by his parents help Clancy's situation? Was it enough for him or did he want more?
- Why did Clancy sneak into the Hereford's field?
- When all the cows decided to pull down the fence separating them, what happened?
- Can you think of any fences we could pull down in our classroom that would help build more positive relationships?

Other suitable titles:

"Musical Chairs" is a short story in *Hot Issues, Cool Choices* by Sandra McLeod Humphrey (2007). Questions are provided at the conclusion of the story for class discussion and personal reflection.

Activity—Y Chart for Equality and Exclusion

Arrange the students in groups of three to four, and give each group two poster boards. Ask the students to draw a large Y on both sheets and write *Equality* on one and *Exclusion* on the other in large letters. Explain that each group will use these sheets to describe how equality and exclusion look, sound, and feel.

The following completed example can be shared with the students once they have completed their Y charts. Discuss and display the finished equality chart as a reminder to students of actions they can take to include others.

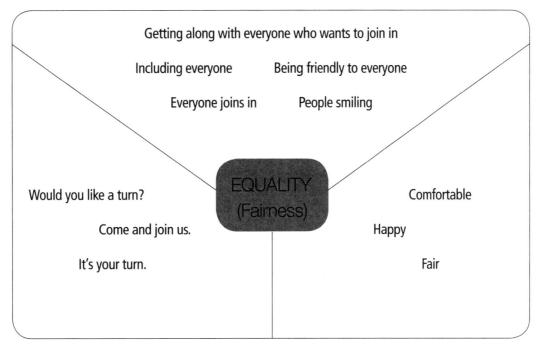

Figure 5: Equality and exclusion Y chart.

Developing Key Messages

Activity—Shape Town

Read the "Shape Town" story to the students using the "Shape Town" resource sheet. At the end of the story, give each group of three to four students an envelope containing only the straight-edged shapes (not the circle) from the shape wall (cut out from the "Template for Shape Wall" resource sheet). Ask the students in each group to take one piece each and try to build the wall with their group. (Hint: The wall is in a rectangular shape.)

When all the pieces are put together correctly, the wall will look like the following.

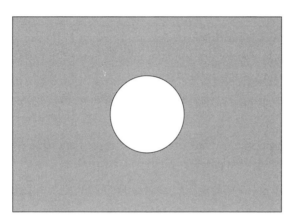

The students will realize the shapes from Shape Town need the circle to complete the wall to stop the water from flooding their town. They realize that it takes all sorts of different individuals to make a community. Ask students to discuss in their group to decide how they could approach the circle and what they could say to ask for his help. Ask each group to role-play their actions and words for the class.

Discuss the importance of cooperation in this situation and how it is important to include all people regardless of their differences.

This story can also be used to focus on the importance of resolution and to reinforce that saying sorry is just one part of resolving a conflict. The next step is to ensure that the conflict is resolved in a positive way and friendships are restored.

Reflecting on Key Messages

Student Journal

Students reflect and write a short paragraph about how they can be more understanding of other people's differences and try to make an effort to include people who are being excluded.

Teacher Reflection

How effectively were the key messages developed?

To what extent are your students now able to:

- Identify fairness, equality, and exclusion in groups?
- Describe behaviors and attitudes that reflect treating people fairly and equally?
- Demonstrate fostering a culture of fairness and equality within our school community?

Section 3

Focus 3: Empathy—Understanding How Others Feel

Key Messages

Understanding how others feel can help us see situations from another person's point of view.

Understanding how others feel is important in all relationships both online and offline.

This focus will enable students to:

- Identify times when they need to try to understand how others may be feeling
- Predict how others may be feeling
- Apply strategies to demonstrate their understanding of others' feelings

Focus 3 Activities	Resources Needed
Introducing Key Messages	
Literature	A text that provides an example of showing empathy (Sample text: *The Big Little Book of Happy Sadness* by Colin Thompson, 2009)
Do you feel what they feel?	Photos, newspaper clippings, magazine pictures
Developing Key Messages	
Feelings Charades	Resource sheet: "Feelings Charades"
Shoe Shuffle	Resource sheet: "Shoe Shuffle"
Reflecting on Key Messages	
Journal	Journal, writing materials

Introducing Key Messages

Explain to students that to have empathy is to understand how another person may be feeling (it can be like putting yourself in his or her shoes). By trying to understand how others may be feeling we can better appreciate why they are feeling or behaving the way that they are. If you have been bullied or excluded at school, then you can better understand how another person feels when the same thing happens to him or her. Understanding how someone feels and trying to make him or her feel better help you to be a good friend and encourage other people to empathize with you too.

By recognizing that someone might be in pain either physically or emotionally and responding in a kind way, for example, asking him or her if he or she is OK and if you can help, we are expressing our empathy. When people have empathy for each other, they can help each other get better.

Explain that showing empathy is not restricted to times when people are sad. We can recognize when someone is feeling fantastic about something and give him or her a pat on the back or a thumbs up, to show we understand how good he or she is feeling and that we want to share that joy.

Explain that if we have an understanding of how we feel about something, it will help us have a better understanding of how others feel about the same or similar things. It would be quite easy to display empathy to others if, when we asked them, they simply told us how they were feeling. However, telling others how we feel is not always easy, and so we need to be detectives and use other clues to try and work out how people feel. Looking at someone's eyes, facial expression, posture, and body language can be useful ways to find out how he or she is feeling. You might look at someone and notice that his or her eyes are not sparkling as they usually do, or he or she may be sitting at his or her desk hunched over, when normally he or she would be sitting taller and looking interested in what is going on around the classroom. This may mean that the student is feeling sad about something. If a student in your class is feeling really excited, you may notice he or she is energetic and jumping around and smiling a lot.

Some reasons why we need to try to be empathic to others include:

- Not judging others and their actions before considering why they may be acting that way
- Being able to understand and care for others who may not be as fortunate physically, emotionally, or socially as you
- Not putting your thoughts and feelings above the thoughts and feelings of others to increase your self-esteem
- Being able to offer opinions in discussions because you are able to see other sides of a situation
- Developing a greater capacity to respond in a more positive way to conflict in friendships

Teacher note: The best way for students to gain an understanding of empathy is the role modeling they are exposed to on a daily basis by their parents, guardians, and teachers. We can explain and give students many examples of empathy, but what they will remember most is the way they see us behave in certain situations. This is a good time to reflect on the levels of empathy displayed to all members of your school. TV shows also provide teachable moments for students to see when and how characters show empathy.

Section 3

Literature

Choose and read a text that provides an example of showing empathy. Initiate a class discussion using the following questions.

- How was the person feeling?
- Why was he or she feeling that way?
- What actions were taken to demonstrate empathy?

Example Using *The Big Little Book of Happy Sadness* by Colin Thompson (2009)

This story beautifully illustrates a young boy's capacity to feel empathy for a dog in the local dog shelter, who feels as lonely and sad as he does. Convincing his grandmother to let him take the dog home brings much happiness to the three main characters in the book. The book carries a message that we need to act on our empathy for others, not just think about it.

Follow-up questions:

- What did George and the dog in the shelter have in common?
- Why did George feel lonelier on weekends?
- How did George's grandmother feel when George told her about Jeremy the dog?
- Why didn't the empty place in George feel so empty anymore?

Other suitable titles:

Wilfrid Gordon McDonald Partridge by Mem Fox (2009)

The Indian in the Cupboard by Lynne Reid Banks (2001)

Activity—Do You Feel What They Feel?

Ask the students to collect and bring in emotive photos, newspaper clippings, and magazine pictures. Some examples may be photos of families who have lost their homes in a fire, someone who is injured as a result of a car crash, or someone who has won a medal for bravery. In groups of three, ask the students to choose several pictures or photographs to study and discuss how their chosen image makes them feel. Ask the students to identify any images they feel more deeply about than others and to explain the reason for this. Review with the students some of the benefits of being empathic and the positive effect it can have on friendships when understanding how others are feeling.

Developing Key Messages

Activity—Feelings Charades

Copy, cut, and laminate cards from the "Feelings Charades" resource sheet. Stack the cards into a deck and ask a student to select one card. Ask the student to act out the feeling written on the card by using the body language and voice described on the card. Ask the class to guess what feeling the student is portraying. Explain to students that they may ask, "How are you?" and "What are you doing?" No matter what his or her card says, the "character" must answer: "Yeah, I'm OK, thanks" and "Oh, you know, nothing much." That is, he or she must not describe how he or she is acting in words. Characters must instead display their feeling through the way they use their voice and body language. For example, a character who feels confident will look the person asking in the eye and answer strongly. A character who feels nervous will look at his or her feet and his or her voice will shake. Explain to the character he or she must allow the rest of the class to guess how he or she is feeling. Invite other students to take turns acting as the character.

Activity—Shoe Shuffle

Ask students to take off their shoes and put them in the center of the room. Copy and cut enough copies of the "Shoe Shuffle" resource sheet to place one card in each shoe. Ask students to select a pair of shoes (other than their own) and pretend to step into the shoes as they read each card. Ask the students to describe (using words and actions) to a partner what it would feel like to be in this person's shoes. If the students finish before others, ask them to script their own scenarios on the blank cards provided, place them in their partner's shoes, and repeat the exercise.

Section 3

Reflecting on Key Messages

Student Journal

Ask students to describe a time they felt they really understood how someone was feeling because they had similar experiences or to write short answers to the following questions.

- How understanding am I of other people's feelings?
- What are some ways I can be more considerate of other people's feelings in a face-to-face environment?
- What are some ways that I can be more considerate of other people's feelings in an online environment?

Teacher Reflection

How effectively were the key messages developed?

To what extent are your students now able to:

- Identify times when they need to try to understand how others may be feeling?
- Predict how others may be feeling?
- Apply strategies to demonstrate their understanding of others' feelings?

Chapter 17

Relationship Skills

Positive Relationship Skills

Relationship skills help us to deal with relationship problems and other social conflicts. These skills include:

- Making friends and maintaining healthy relationships
- Dealing effectively with negative social influences and conflicts
- Seeking help if we are not able to solve a social problem ourselves

Key Area 4: Relationship Skills

Teacher note: Students should watch the movie or read the book *A Bug's Life* (Anderson, Reher, & Lasseter, 1998; Korman & Fontes, 1998) before beginning any of the activities in this key area.

Focus	This Focus Will Enable Students to:	Focus Activities
1. Behaviors that are bullying	• Identify bullying behaviors • Describe the characteristics of bullying behavior • Demonstrate actions they can take and who they can go to for help in a bullying situation	• Is this bullying? • Heads and Tails game • Y chart and mind map • Literature • What goes on here? • Journal
2. Who is involved in bullying?	• Identify who is involved in bullying situations • Describe the roles of the key players involved in a bullying situation • Demonstrate safe actions key players can take to reduce bullying	• Discussion • *A Bug's Life* • Character study • Journal
3. Why some people bully but most people don't	• Identify reasons some people bully but most people don't • Describe how they feel about bullying behavior • Demonstrate positive alternatives to inappropriate, antisocial, and bullying behavior	• What do I do? • Mind mapping • "A Tale of Two Boys" • Journal
4. Bystanders to bullying	• Identify the decisions a bystander can make when he or she sees bullying, including cyberbullying • Describe the role of the bystander and the influence he or she can have on bullying situations • Demonstrate safe, positive bystander actions in bullying situations	• Literature • Jigsaw • Journal

Key Area 4: Relationship Skills

Positive Relationship Skills

Focus 1: Behaviors That Are Bullying

Key Messages

Bullying is a repeated behavior that may be physical, verbal, or psychological, in which there is *intent* to *cause fear, distress,* or *harm* to another, that is conducted by a *more powerful* individual or group against a *less powerful* individual or group of individuals *unable to stop this* from happening.

Cyberbullying is when over a period of time an individual or a group uses information and communication technology to intentionally harm a person who finds it hard to stop this bullying from happening.

This focus will enable students to:

- Identify bullying behaviors
- Describe the characteristics of bullying behavior
- Demonstrate actions they can take and who they can go to for help in a bullying situation

Section 3

Focus 1 Activities	Resources Needed
Introducing Key Messages	
Is this bullying?	Resource sheet: "Types of Bullying"
Heads and Tails	
Developing Key Messages	
Y chart and mind maps	Paper, felt-tip pens
Literature	A text that provides an example of bullying (Sample text: *My Secret Bully* by Trudy Ludwig, 2005)
What goes on here?	Activity sheet: "What Goes on Here?"
Reflecting on Key Messages	
Journal	Journal, writing materials

Introducing Key Messages

Discuss with students the difference between *overt* and *covert* bullying (obvious and not-so-obvious) and explain how cyberbullying is an example of covert bullying. Discuss how being covertly bullied is a common experience among students, and the tendency to bully in covert rather than overt ways increases with age. Ask the students to write their own definitions of bullying (including cyberbullying) and share these with the class.

Use the "Types of Bullying" resource sheet to familiarize students with the following definitions.

Bullying is a repeated behavior used by a more powerful person to intentionally cause fear, distress, or harm to a less powerful person who cannot stop the bullying from happening.

Some types of bullying include:

Exclusion
- Ignoring others, leaving others out on purpose, or not allowing them to join in either online or offline

Physical bullying
- Hitting, kicking, or pushing others around

Lies or rumors
- Telling lies or nasty stories about someone to make other students dislike him or her. This can be offline or online, for example, via a social networking site, email, or mobile phone.

Threats
- Making someone afraid that he or she will be hurt, either offline or online
- Staring or giving someone mean looks or gestures
- Forcing someone to do things he or she doesn't want to

Hurtful teasing and verbal abuse
- Making fun of and teasing others in a mean and hurtful way, either offline or online

Cyberbullying
- When an individual or group uses the Internet, mobile phones, or other technology to intentionally hurt another person or group of people

Activity—Is This Bullying?

Discuss how it is not always easy to know whether a behavior is bullying or not. Sometimes students are just messing around, but at some point their actions may become deliberately hurtful or bullying. The following list will help students understand the implications of their actions a little more. Discuss with students how the following questions can help them figure out if they are engaging in bullying behavior.

- Are my actions or words deliberately hurting someone else's feelings?
- Are my actions deliberately hurting someone else physically?
- Are my actions or words deliberately making someone else feel afraid?
- Am I deliberately trying to control someone else?
- Am I unfairly taking out my feelings of anger or frustration on someone else?
- Would I like someone else to do this to me?
- How would I feel if someone deliberately did this to me again and again?

Activity—Heads and Tails

Explain to the students how to play the Heads and Tails game.

Heads: Two hands on head indicate a bullying situation.

Tails: Two hands on tails (base of spine) indicate a not very nice behavior but not a bullying situation.

Head and tail: One hand on head and one hand on tail indicate *neither a* bullying situation nor a behavior problem—an accident, joking around, or nothing to worry about.

Explain you are going to read some scenarios and ask the students to classify these as bullying or not bullying by using their heads and tails. It is important to include bullying situations that have happened in the school. Ask selected students to explain the reasons behind their decision. Highlight the scenarios in which students vote differently and discuss the reasons for this. Invite the students to supply some scenarios of their own, and ask the class to vote. Encourage the students to discuss why bullying in any form is an unacceptable behavior.

- A fourth-grade boy is running to get to the playground at lunchtime. As he runs around a corner, he collides with and knocks over a first-grade girl. She is upset; however, the fourth-grade boy is in such a hurry to get to the playground he doesn't notice and keeps on running.
- A fifth-grade girl pinches another fifth-grade girl on the arm every time she walks past her in the classroom. The pinches hurt, and she is now afraid to walk by the other student.
- Students in a group who have always been your friends start leaving you out when they are talking online to each other, and you don't know why.

- A boy comes to school with a new haircut and says to a friend, "Look what my mom did to my hair." The friend replies, "You look like an echidna; let's go find you some insects to eat for lunch," and they both burst out laughing together.
- A student in your class posts lots of nasty messages on his Facebook account about the clothes you wore to school and what other students thought about you.
- You play soccer at lunchtime every day. When you check your mobile phone for messages after school, there is always one from another student saying that you are a complete loser at soccer and that if you keep turning up to the lunchtime game, you will be sorry.
- You are part of a group at school and play together every day. The same students are in your after-school basketball team; however, they always completely ignore you at training and pretend they don't know you.

Developing Key Messages

Activity—Y Chart and Mind Maps

Arrange the students into groups of three or four. Give each group a sheet of butcher paper and a felt-tip pen. Assign each group one of the forms of bullying: exclusion, physical bullying, lies or rumors, threats, hurtful teasing and verbal abuse, or cyberbullying.

Ask each group to write its allocated form of bullying in the middle of a Y chart on the paper provided. The students illustrate or find pictures of each form of bullying and glue these onto the charts.

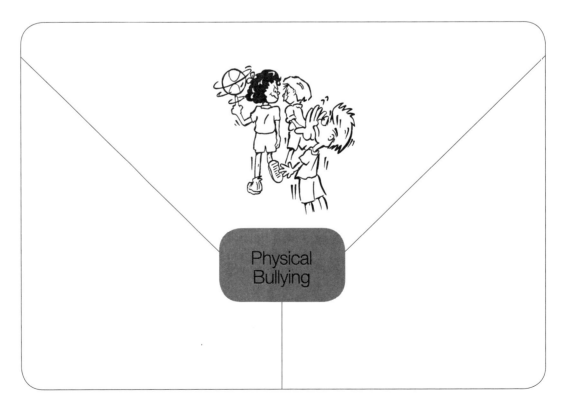

Figure 6: Bullying Y chart.

Each group completes the "Looks like," "Sounds like," and "Feels like" sections of its chart, and then reports its findings to the class. Ask the students to define what each behavior involves; for example, if a student suggests the silent treatment as a form of bullying, he or she can define what the silent treatment is and what kind of bullying it is, such as, the silent treatment is when someone refuses to talk to you. This is a form of exclusion because it is deliberately leaving someone out.

Alternatively, ask the students to create a mind map based around the question "Exclusion—What is it and how does it feel?"

Invite the students to display their mind maps, and allow time for comments and discussion from the class.

Literature

Choose and read a text that provides an example of bullying. Initiate a class discussion using the following questions.

- What type of bullying did we see evidence of?
- How did the bullying behavior affect others?
- What positive actions were taken to stop the bullying?
- What would you have done in this situation?

Example Using *My Secret Bully* by Trudy Ludwig (2005)

This picture book makes reference to all three participants in a bullying situation: the person who bullies, the person who is being bullied, and the bystander. While the title refers specifically to relational aggression, it clearly highlights the effects of bullying and the need to provide students who are targets of bullying with strategies to deal with bullying situations. It also encourages students to look at what is going on from the perspective of all three participants. Fourth grade appears to be a grade in which relational aggression becomes more evident than in previous grades, particularly with girls, although this form of bullying is not gender specific.

My Secret Bully contains some excellent discussion questions at the end of the book to help students draw parallels between this story and situations they or their friends may have experienced in school.

Follow-up questions:

- Who can you ask for help if you are being bullied?
- What can you do if you see someone being bullied?
- Why is bullying an unacceptable behavior? Why is cyberbullying an unacceptable behavior?

Section 3

Activity—What Goes on Here?

Give each student a copy of the "What Goes on Here?" activity sheet. Ask students to add to the list of types of bullying behaviors described on the sheet and indicate with a tick how often they think this type of behavior occurs in their school. Encourage the students to include face-to-face (offline) and cyberbullying (online) examples. Compare the completed sheets and look for similarities and differences in the students' responses to the types and frequency of bullying in their school. Discuss these with the students.

Reflecting on Key Messages

Student Journal

Describe a bullying situation you have seen.

- What type of bullying was it?
- How did it make you feel?
- What did you do?
- How did you feel about the person who was doing the bullying?
- If this happened again, what would you do and who would you ask for help?

Teacher Reflection

How effectively were the key messages developed?

To what extent are your students now able to:

- Identify bullying behaviors?
- Describe the characteristics of bullying behavior?
- Demonstrate actions they can take and who they can go to for help in a bullying situation?

Focus 2: Who Is Involved in Bullying?

Key Messages

There is always more than one person involved in a bullying situation.
Everyone can take action to reduce bullying.

This focus will enable students to:

- Identify who is involved in bullying situations
- Describe the roles of the key players involved in a bullying situation
- Demonstrate safe actions key players can take to reduce bullying

Focus 2 Activities	Resources Needed
Introducing Key Messages	
Discussion	
A Bug's Life	*A Bug's Life* book or DVD (Anderson et al., 1998; Korman & Fontes, 1998)
Developing Key Messages	
Character study	Activity sheet: "Character Study"
Reflecting on Key Messages	
Journal	Journal, writing materials

Introducing Key Messages

Explain to the students that when bullying occurs in the school environment it can affect many people, not just the people directly involved in the bullying situation. Explain that while most students are not directly involved in bullying, many can be affected as bystanders. As bystanders, students have the opportunity to play a very important role in the prevention of bullying, for example, by offering assistance to students who are bullied, seeking help by telling someone what is happening, and influencing their peer group to refrain from bullying others. Discuss how learning to recognize the role they play in a bullying situation will help them to determine what actions they need to take to reduce bullying in your school.

Section 3

Discussion

Discuss the following diagram, which describes the roles of key players involved in a bullying situation.

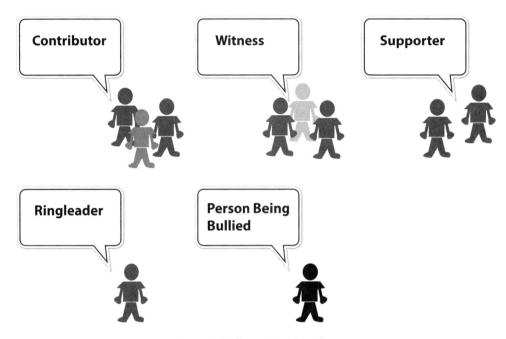

Figure 7: Bullying situation chart.

- *A person who bullies (ringleader)*: This person intentionally tries to hurt another person again and again.
- *A person who is being bullied*: This person is deliberately made to feel fear and distress or is physically or emotionally hurt by a more powerful person or group and is unable to stop it from happening.
- *Bystander*: This person sees the bullying or knows that it is happening to someone else. There may be bystanders who are afraid they may be bullied next, and this may influence their decision about what they will do if they see bullying happening. There are different types of bystanders, and in this model, the bystanders are described in the following categories.
- *Contributor*: This person offers support to the person bullying, either by helping the person to bully the other person or by encouraging the person bullying. This person might gather to watch the incident (sometimes from concern for the person being bullied, sometimes to see what will happens, and sometimes for enjoyment).
  - *Supporter*: This person dislikes the bullying, is concerned for the person being bullied, and actively tries to help the person being bullied.
  - *Witness*: This person knows the bullying is going on but is not directly involved.

Discuss with students how bystanders may act in many different ways when they see bullying taking place, including:

- Watching what is going on and not getting involved
- Pretending not to see and ignoring the situation
- Choosing to get involved in the bullying
- Choosing to get involved and stop the bullying
- Choosing to get help

Stress to the students that, as bystanders, the way they behave can either contribute to or help to stop bullying. Many students don't know how to help the person being bullied. Discuss the importance of taking only safe actions to help someone who is being bullied. Some of these actions include:

- Letting the person doing the bullying know what he or she is doing is bullying
- Refusing to join in with bullying and walking away
- Asking a teacher or support person for help
- Moving close to the person being bullied and showing him or her that you want to help, even if you are not sure how to go about it
- Being aware of students who are alone and are more likely to be the target of bullying, and trying to include them in what you are doing with your friends

Ask the students to suggest other safe actions they would feel comfortable taking to help someone who is being bullied and display these in a prominent place for students to be able to refer to. Ask students if the actions they suggest would change according to who was carrying out the bullying behavior and who was being bullied. If yes, ask them to explain why.

Activity—*A Bug's Life*

Show the students the DVD or read a shortened version of the story *A Bug's Life*. This story depicts the roles of key people involved in a bullying situation. The grasshoppers bully the ants every year to make the ants collect their food. The leader of the grasshoppers, Hopper, behaves meanly and does not care about how the ants feel or what happens to them as long as he gets his supply of food. The other grasshoppers are the bystanders who support the leader to get their share of the food and because they are scared of him. One ant stands up to the grasshoppers and shows the others that if they support each other they can overcome the bullying. One scene in the movie shows the lead grasshopper explaining to the other grasshoppers what could happen if the ants united to stop the bullying behavior. This is one of the most important scenes in the story for this activity. Discuss how when the ants (bystanders) joined together to support Flik, the grasshoppers (contributing bystanders) ran away and no longer supported Hopper (ringleader). He lost his power over the ants when the bystanders weren't supporting him.

Section 3

Developing Key Messages

Activity—Character Study

After viewing the movie or reading the book *A Bug's Life*, ask students to use the "Character Study" activity sheet. Identify the main characters and their roles in each of the following bullying situations.

- Flik being bullied by Hopper with the other grasshoppers standing behind Hopper as contributors, and then the other ants behind the grasshoppers as witnesses
- Flik trying to convince the other ants to take action to stop Hopper
- Hopper explaining to the other grasshoppers why they must go back and continue to bully the ants
- Flik stepping up to help Dot when she was being bullied by Hopper and the other grasshoppers
- The Queen stepping up to help Flik when he was hurt
- All the other ants showing their agitation when the Queen was being threatened

Discuss with the students the actions the bystanders in the movie or story took to stop the bullying, once they recognized that they could do something as a group.

Characters	Ringleader	Bullied	Contributor	Supporter
Hopper				
Other grasshoppers				
Flik		✓		
Queen		✓		✓
Princess Atta				✓
Dot				
Circus bugs				

Ask the students to identify a TV show or movie they have watched where bullying is portrayed using the "TV Show or Movie" chart on the "Character Study" activity sheet. Students fill in character names and match them to the bystander roles. Select students to tell the class about the TV show or movie they have chosen. Ask students to discuss and suggest what actions bystanders could take to help reduce the bullying seen in these TV shows and movies.

Arrange students in groups of three or four, and ask them to brainstorm ways they could encourage all students to stand up against bullying, for example, hosting a purple ribbon day in which all students wear a purple ribbon to show total school support against bullying behavior. Compile a list of all suggestions, and ask students to vote on which activity they would like to implement in their school. Help students to plan and implement this day.

Reflecting on Key Messages

Student Journal

Ask the students to recall a bullying incident they have observed happening online or offline, where they took no action to help the person being bullied. Ask students to write a story about this situation, giving it a different ending and writing what actions as a bystander they would take to help the person being bullied and to stop the bullying behavior from continuing.

Teacher Reflection

How effectively were the key messages developed?

To what extent are your students now able to:

- Identify who is involved in bullying situations?
- Describe the roles of the key players involved in a bullying situation?
- Demonstrate safe actions key players can take to reduce bullying?

Section 3

Focus 3: Why Some People Bully but Most People Don't

Key Messages

Most students do not bully other students at school.

Students who are nice to others are much more fun to be around than those who bully.

This focus will enable students to:

- Identify reasons some people bully but most people don't
- Describe how they feel about bullying behavior
- Demonstrate positive alternatives to inappropriate, antisocial, and bullying behavior

Focus 3 Activities	Resources Needed
Introducing Key Messages	
What do I do?	Activity sheet: "What Do I Do?"
	Resource sheet: "How Do I Avoid Bullying Others?"
Developing Key Messages	
Mind mapping	Paper, drawing and writing materials
"A Tale of Two Boys"	
Reflecting on Key Messages	
Journal	Journal, writing materials

Introducing Key Messages

Discuss how some people think students who misbehave or who have problems at school are the students who bully. Explain that this is not always the case, as some students who bully are popular with good leadership skills. They can have groups of friends and the support of this group. They can also be popular with the teachers and can be well-behaved in class. Talk about how sometimes people don't realize that what they are doing is bullying behavior and don't realize how much their bullying behavior is affecting others.

Discuss with students reasons why some people bully others. Some reasons include:

- As a leader of a group he or she thinks bullying is part of what to do.
- They think this is the best way to get what they want.
- It makes them feel more powerful than other people.
- They feel jealous of other people and the attention they get.
- They think it makes them look tough.
- They think it makes them popular and people will want to be their friend.
- They have noticed it work for other people and think it might work for them too.
- They are being bullied and have decided to bully others, too.

Ask students to suggest other reasons why some people bully and to identify which of the preceding reasons seem to be the most common for cyberbullying versus face-to-face bullying.

Explain to the students how people often bully others because they have learned that it is a way to feel powerful and to get what they want. However, because this behavior is learned, it can also be *unlearned*.

Discuss why most people do not bully others. Encourage students to consider the following reasons.

- They have good social skills.
- They think bullying is wrong.
- They don't feel the need to bully.
- They are too busy to think about it.
- They have strong, supportive friendship groups.
- They believe that bullying is not worth it.

Ask students to suggest other reasons they believe most students do not bully.

Activity—What Do I Do?

Hand each student a copy of the "What Do I Do?" activity sheet, and display an enlarged copy of the "How Do I Avoid Bullying Others?" resource sheet. Read and discuss each situation with students. Explain that sometimes we say things without thinking about the consequences of our words. Ask students to refer to the "How Do I Avoid Bullying Others?" resource sheet, and decide on positive actions they could take to make each situation better.

Developing Key Messages

Activity—Mind Mapping

Explain to students that mind mapping is a way of visually recording information about a topic. It is a more interesting way of presenting thoughts and ideas. Explain that one of the best things about mind maps is that no two maps are alike. Using different pens, pencils, markers, text, connecting lines, and pictures helps to make every mind map unique to the person who created it and makes it easier for him or her to recall what his or her mind map is about.

Explain that mind maps usually begin with a single word or picture in the center of a large piece of paper. Lines are then drawn from this word or picture and more information added to each line. The mind map that follows is an example of reasons people bully.

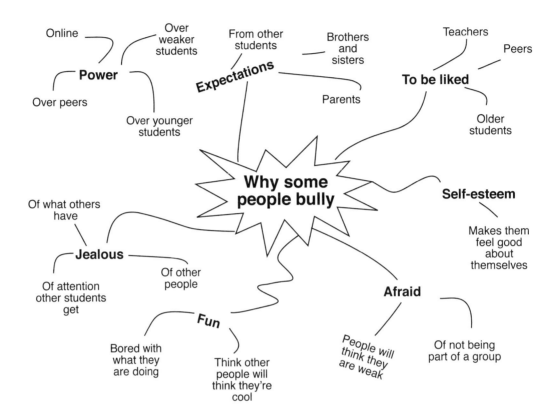

Figure 8: Why some people bully mind map.

Explain that the information we have gathered so far in this lesson on why some people bully others and why most people do not bully others could have been represented as a mind map. Ask students to construct their own mind maps on types of bullying, including cyberbullying. Remind students that people who cyberbully others also often bully others face-to-face and people who are cyberbullied are often also bullied face-to-face. Reinforce with students the differences between *covert* and *overt* types of bullying and the possible motivation behind these types of bullying. As a class, compare these mind maps.

- What features do the mind maps have in common?
- How are the mind maps different?
- What conclusions, if any, can we draw from this?

Activity—"A Tale of Two Boys"

Read to students the following story: "A Tale of Two Boys."

> **A Tale of Two Boys**
>
> There was a boy who used to be in my class who was suspended for bullying. His name was James. He was normally very quiet, and no one really paid much attention to him.
>
> One day at lunchtime another boy in my class named Greg was showing off with a hacky sack. A few kids had gathered around to watch him, including James. One time, James pushed Greg lightly so he missed the hacky sack. It was just a joke and a few people laughed, even Greg. James seemed to like the attention so he did it again and again. More people gathered around, and James started pushing Greg really hard.
>
> Finally, Greg actually fell and cut his arm. Greg started crying, and more and more people gathered around. They weren't laughing anymore, and some told James to stop. But he seemed to like the attention even if it was for doing the wrong thing. James started calling Greg names and telling him to get up so he could push him down again. Eventually, a teacher saw what was happening and intervened. James was suspended from school for a week.
>
> When James came back he seemed very embarrassed. He realized what he had done to Greg was very wrong. Nobody wanted to talk to him. James apologized to Greg but always felt badly about how he had treated him. I think James made a big mistake bullying Greg.

Arrange students in pairs, and ask each pair to consider the following questions.

- Why did James bully?
- What could James have done instead of bullying if he wasn't feeling good about himself?
- Describe how James seemed to be feeling at the time.
- Describe how James felt about Greg at the time he was bullying him.
- What actions could have been taken (and by whom) to help Greg and James?
- Describe how James felt about the situation after he realized how much he had hurt Greg.
- Describe how the other students felt about James.

Ask students to retell the story in pairs, role-playing words and actions Greg and the bystanders could have taken to change the outcome. For example:

1. Greg says, "Stop it, I don't like it."
2. Bystanders step in to protect Greg or help Greg before he is pushed over.
3. James realizes he has hurt Greg and helps Greg up and apologizes.

Teacher note: Do not allow students to role-play James when he is bullying.

Section 3

Reflecting on Key Messages

Student Journal

Ask students to answer the following questions in their journals.

- What safe actions can I take as a bystander if I see someone being bullied face-to-face?
- What safe actions can I take as a bystander if I see someone being cyberbullied on a social networking site like Club Penguin or Moshi Monsters?

Teacher Reflection

How effectively were the key messages developed?

To what extent are your students now able to:

- Identify reasons why some people bully but most people don't?
- Describe how they feel about bullying behavior?
- Demonstrate positive alternatives to inappropriate, antisocial, and bullying behavior?

Focus 4: Bystanders to Bullying

Key Messages

Bystanders are people who know bullying is happening because they have seen or heard about it.

Bystanders can choose safe ways to help a person being bullied.

By taking no action, bystanders contribute to the bullying.

This focus will enable students to:

- Identify the decisions a bystander can make when he or she sees bullying, including cyberbullying
- Describe the role of the bystander and the influence he or she can have on bullying situations
- Demonstrate safe, positive bystander actions in bullying situations

Focus 4 Activities	Resources Needed
Introducing Key Messages	
Literature	A text that provides an example of the bystander's role in a bullying situation
	(Sample text: *Nobody Knew What to Do: A Story About Bullying* by Becky Ray McCain, 2001)
Developing Key Messages	
Jigsaw	Paper, felt-tip pen, cards
Reflecting on Key Messages	
Journal	Journal, writing materials

Introducing Key Messages

Discuss how bullying involves more than just the students who are bullied and those who bully. Research shows that peers have been observed to be involved in 85 percent of bullying episodes, with the involvement ranging from actively participating to just observing. Peers are also likely to be present during most bullying incidents at school.

As bystanders, peers can influence the bullying behavior through their own behavior by moving away or intervening to stop the bullying. Bystanders' influence can be used in a positive way to protect the person being bullied and to motivate students who bully to change their behavior.

Most students strongly believe in fairness and want to be part of programs and activities that encourage students to treat others fairly.

Once students are mobilized to take action against bullying, they must feel secure that teachers understand their need to stay safe. For some students this means ensuring that the information they share will not cause them to lose status in their peer group.

Explain to students that by mobilizing positive peer influence against bullying behavior, students who are bullied will feel supported and more confident in applying the skills they have learned in all areas of the school environment.

Refer students to Figure 7: "Bullying Situation Chart" on page 184, which indicates the roles of key players involved in a bullying situation. Ask the students to define the characteristics of each person in the model and the part each plays in a bullying situation.

Reinforce with students that as bystanders they are key to discouraging bullying in their school. Students usually know what is going on among other students and who the bullying students are before adults do. Explain to students the importance of knowing who to go to for help if they feel worried or unsure of what to do in a bullying situation.

Literature

Choose and read a text that provides an example of the bystander's role in a bullying situation. Conduct a guided discussion to identify the different characters and the roles they played in the bullying situation.

Arrange the students in small groups and assign a character to each member of the group. Allow time for the students to practice role-playing actions they could take when the bullying occurs. *Be sure to make it clear to students they are not to role-play bullying behavior.* Students present their responses to the rest of the class.

Example Using *Nobody Knew What to Do: A Story About Bullying* by Becky Ray McCain (2001)

This picture book addresses how views on dealing with bullying are changing, and that as a society, we believe it is no longer acceptable to stand by and do nothing when we see another person being bullied. The story highlights the fear and uncertainty students feel when they are not sure what to do to help. It also offers some suggestions for actions they can take to tackle this problem. Notes at the back of the book provide some useful information for teachers regarding bullying prevention.

Follow-up questions:

- What other actions could the main character in the book have taken when students started picking on Ray, rather than squeezing his eyes shut and covering his ears?
- If you were the main character in this story, how would you feel when Ray did not come to school?
- If you see someone being bullied, and you can't stop the bullying from happening, who would you go to for help?
- How does asking for help make you feel?

Developing Key Messages

Activity—Jigsaw

Arrange the students in groups of four and supply each group with six cards with one of the following six questions written on each card. Each group member should have a different question card to which they respond. After each group has distributed one of the cards to each group member, it should move to a group of students with that same question, for example, the students with question one should sit together, and the students with question two sit together, and so on. In these larger groups, the students as a group determine their answers to these questions, and each write the responses collected onto their own piece of paper. After five to ten minutes of brainstorming and recording the groups' responses, the students move back to their original groups of four with the responses they collected. In these groups of four, they should assemble all the information they collected and use the best of this information to prepare a poster. This poster should encourage young people to take positive action if they see someone being bullied and explain why they should do this.

Questions:

1. What can you say to discourage someone who is bullying someone else?
2. What type of body language can you use to discourage someone who is bullying someone else?
3. How can you keep yourself safe when you are helping someone else who is being bullied?
4. What can you do to specifically help someone who is being cyberbullied; for example, what types of messages could you send them?
5. Who could you try to get help from if you knew someone was being bullied?
6. What kind of help does someone who is being bullied need from his or her peers?

Display the finished posters for students to refer to when confronted with bullying situations. Reinforce with students the need to be safe at all times as a bystander and that if they are unsure how to respond, they should always ask a trusted person for help.

Reflecting on Key Messages

Student Journal

Ask students to respond to the following prompts in their journals.

- Describe ways you may support bullying behavior without realizing you are doing it, for example, by ignoring or remaining silent about bullying behavior.
- Describe ways you may support bullying behavior in an active way, for example, by laughing or smiling at the bullying taking place.
- What skills do you need to develop to have the confidence to support students who are being bullied, for example, being able to empathize with the distress felt by the person being bullied?

Teacher Reflection

How effectively were the key messages developed?

To what extent are your students now able to:

- Identify the decisions a bystander can make when he or she sees bullying, including cyberbullying?
- Describe the role of the bystander and the influence he or she can have on bullying situations?
- Demonstrate safe, positive bystander actions in bullying situations?

Chapter 18

Social Decision Making

Social Information Processing

STEWART HAD BADLY MISJUDGED THE SOCIAL EXPECTATIONS IN THE PIG-PEN

Social decision-making skills help us consider the consequences of our actions for ourselves and others and make thoughtful, sensible decisions. This involves:

- Understanding how a social situation makes us feel
- Considering the different choices we have and the positive and negative consequences of each of these choices when making a decision
- Making positive choices while considering how these choices may affect ourselves and others

Section 3

197

Key Area 5: Social Decision Making

Focus	This Focus Will Enable Students to:	Focus Activities
1. Taking steps to help solve social problems	• Identify times when they can safely take action to discourage bullying as a bystander to a bullying situation • Describe the steps involved in the decision-making model • Demonstrate, using the decision-making model, that they can decide how to deal with bullying behavior	• Investigating the model • A boy, a ball, and bullying behavior • From model to action • Journal

Key Area 5: Social Decision Making

Social Information Processing

Focus 1: Taking Steps to Help Solve Social Problems

Key Messages

Sometimes the actions we choose to deal with bullying don't always provide the response we want.

If the bullying continues we need to go back to our decision-making model and choose another action to try.

Sometimes we need to tell someone who will listen and help us with our decision-making process.

This focus will enable students to:

- Identify times when they can safely take action to discourage bullying as a bystander to a bullying situation
- Describe the steps involved in the decision-making model
- Demonstrate, using the decision-making model, that they can decide how to deal with bullying behavior

Focus 1 Activities	Resources Needed
Introducing Key Messages	
Investigating the model	Cardboard
Developing Key Messages	
A boy, a ball, and bullying behavior	Story
From model to action	Activity sheet: "Bullying Situation Cards" Resource sheet: "Decision-Making Model"
Reflecting on Key Messages	
Journal	Journal, writing materials

Introducing Key Messages

Remind the students how many decisions we make every day, from the time we get up until the time we go to bed. Some decisions are simple and might include when to get up, what to have for breakfast, who to play with at recess or lunchtime, and whether to complete our school work.

Some decisions we make affect only ourselves, while others have consequences for others as well. We need to always try to make sure that important decisions are well considered, especially when there is a level of harm or risk involved.

Activity—Investigating the Model

Display the following words written individually on large pieces of cardboard:

> STOP   FEEL   THINK   DECIDE   PLAN   DO

Explain to the students that these words represent the steps involved in the decision-making model. In pairs, ask the students to discuss and write the words on a piece of paper in the order they would choose for the decision-making model to be most effective. Ask each group to explain the reasons for their order. Rearrange the words on the board as the STOP, FEEL, THINK, DECIDE, PLAN, DO model. Explain that students are going to investigate each step of the model to help them decide what to do as a bystander, when they want to help someone who is being bullied, while at the same time making sure they are not putting themselves at risk.

Brainstorm words and phrases associated with each step of the model, for example:

- Under *STOP* students may write that they'll stand still to assess what is happening.
- Under *FEEL* students may write how they might be feeling about what is going on.
- Under *THINK* students may work out what is going on.

Display the results around the words on the board. Divide the classroom in half with a piece of masking tape. Explain to students that you are going to read out a series of statements

Section 3

(such as the following). If the students agree with the statement, they move to the left-hand side of the tape; if they disagree, they move to the right-hand side of the tape. Randomly select students to explain why they agreed or disagreed, and ask them to explain reasons for their answers.

- The way you feel about a situation is influenced by your values.
- All the choices you make have consequences.
- These consequences can be positive or negative.
- Deciding what to do can be difficult.
- Formulating a clear plan will help you to take action.
- You can use this decision-making model when you see someone being cyberbullied.
- If you see someone being bullied, you don't have to do anything. Let someone else sort it out.
- You do not have to think about the consequences of your actions—just do what you want.
- Everyone should just look out for him- or herself and not worry about what is happening to other people.
- It is OK to leave someone out if he or she is not one of your close friends.

Developing Key Messages

Activity—A Boy, a Ball, and Bullying Behavior

Discuss how this activity will be conducted as Reader's Theater. Choose six students to play the characters in the story. The part of the narrator is played by the teacher. Have a set of cardboard signs with the words STOP, FEEL, THINK, DECIDE, PLAN, DO available to use.

The story is written to help students understand how the Stop, Feel, Think, Decide, Plan, Do decision-making model can be put into practice. Emphasize the need to focus on the consequences—both positive and negative—of each of the bystander's choices and the effects of this on all characters in the story.

Narrator: "Tom, Jessica, Mark, and Sophie were all friends in fourth grade. One day at lunchtime they were sitting in the shade of a big tree next to the basketball courts watching the seventh graders play basketball, when the ball bounced into the window of the spooky old shed. The door was always locked, and the seventh graders couldn't fit through the window.

"One of the seventh graders called out to Tom, and he walked over. The seventh-grade student asked Tom if he would climb through the window and get the ball, because he was small enough to fit, but Tom didn't want to. The teachers had told all the students not to go into the shed because it wasn't safe. The seventh grader started to pressure Tom."

Seventh grader: "What's the matter with you? It's just a shed. Are you scared?"

Tom: "I'm not scared. It's just the teachers don't let us go in there."

Seventh grader: "Well maybe I'll give you something to be scared of."

Narrator: "Tom didn't say anything. He didn't know what to do. The seventh grader grabbed him and began dragging him over to the shed. Jessica, Mark, and Sophie saw it all. They looked at each other and wondered what to do."

Narrator: *[Holds up STOP sign]* "What is going on?"

The narrator asks the students to share what they think is happening before reading the next paragraph.

> **Narrator:** "Tom is in a situation where he does not know what to do. Jessica, Mark and Sophie don't want their friend Tom to have to go into the shed. The teachers said it was unsafe and he might get hurt."

> **Narrator:** *[Holds up FEEL sign]* "How do Jessica, Mark, and Sophie feel about it?"

The narrator asks students to share how they think Jessica, Mark, and Sophie feel before reading the next paragraph.

> **Narrator:** "They feel scared about what might happen to Tom if he goes in the shed and scared about what the seventh-grade boy might do to him if he doesn't go into the shed. The seventh-grade boy is very big and very aggressive. He would probably hurt them next if they tried to stop him."

> **Narrator:** *[Holds up THINK sign]* "What could they do?"

The narrator asks the students to share what they think Jessica, Mark, and Sophie could do in this situation before reading the next sentence.

> **Narrator:** "All three want to help Tom but are unsure how to go about it."

> **Jessica:** *[Holds up DECIDE sign]* "We have to make a choice here. There will be some consequences based on what we decide to do. Are you all in? Come on, let's go help Tom. There are three of us and only the one seventh grader. If he tries to bully us we can support each other."

> **Sophie:** "No way, look at the size of that seventh grader. All Tom has to do is climb through the window, get the ball, and climb back out. It'll only take a minute, and no one has to get hurt."

> **Mark:** "But Tom might get hurt. The shed is unsafe. The door is always locked for a reason. There might be broken glass or spiders or rusty nails. I'm going to go find a teacher."

> **Narrator:** *[Holds up PLAN sign]*

The narrator asks Jessica, Sophie, and Mark to discuss what choices they could make that will support Tom and make sure they are all safe from the bullying behavior of the seventh-grade student. They then share these choices with the rest of the class.

The narrator holds up the DO sign and asks the remainder of the students to form groups of three in which each takes on the role of Jessica, Mark, or Sophie. Allow time for students to practice role-playing how they would respond as a bystander, to Tom's situation. Invite students to present their role plays to the class. Ask students to vote on which response they would feel comfortable using in a similar situation.

Activity—From Model to Action

Display a copy of the "Decision-Making Model" resource sheet. Explain this activity can be completed individually or in pairs. Copy and cut the "Bullying Situation Cards" activity sheet. Provide students with multiple copies of the "Decision-Making Model" resource sheet.

The students choose a scenario card and then work through their STOP, FEEL, THINK, DECIDE, PLAN, DO Decision-Making Model resource sheet. Writing in each box will help students formulate an action plan for each of these situations.

Come together as a class, and ask the students to share their plan with the rest of the class. The class can then provide positive feedback and alternatives to some of the choices suggested.

In each situation, ask students to be clear about the position they are taking. Are they responding as the person being bullied, or is their response based on what they would do if they were the bystander?

Many of the scenario cards used in previous units would also be suitable for this activity. Encourage the students to write their own scenarios based on situations they have previously observed.

Reflecting on Key Messages

Student Journal

Ask students to reflect on and write short answers to the following.

- Is it harder to respond as a bystander when someone is being targeted by cyberbullying behavior? Why or why not?
- Explain in a few sentences what factors influence the decisions students make as a bystander to bullying situations.

Teacher Reflection

How effectively were the key messages developed?

To what extent are your students now able to:

- Identify times when they can safely take action to discourage bullying as a bystander to a bullying situation?
- Describe the steps involved in the decision-making model?
- Demonstrate, using the decision-making model, that they can decide how to deal with bullying behavior?

Appendices

Middle Childhood

Teacher Resource
Ages 8–10

Appendix A: Activity Sheets

Name: _____

Being Bullied

You are being bullied by the same group of students every week. *How does it feel, and what can you do about it?*	You are being bullied by an older student. *How does it feel, and what can you do about it?*
You are being bullied by one of your good friends. *How does it feel, and what can you do about it?*	You are being bullied by your older brother or sister. *How does it feel, and what can you do about it?*
You are being bullied by a student from another school when walking home. *How does it feel, and what can you do about it?*	You are being bullied by other students on the school bus. *How does it feel, and what can you do about it?*
How does it feel, and what can you do about it?	*How does it feel, and what can you do about it?*

Name: _____

Bullying Situation Cards

Situation 1

You see a student putting trash in another student's backpack every day.

How would you feel?

What would you do?

Situation 2

A student sends an email with a nasty picture of you to the class. Some people then send it to other people outside the school.

How would you feel?

What would you do?

Situation 3

A group of students threatens to hurt your group if you don't give up your lunch money each morning or if you tell a teacher.

How would you feel?

What would you do?

Situation 4

A group of students plays basketball every day, but the students refuse to let you join in each time you ask them.

How would you feel?

What would you do?

Situation 5

A group of students writes untrue and very hurtful statements about you and your family on a blog.

How would you feel?

What would you do?

Situation 6

A student keeps taking your pencils and breaking them in half and giving them back while the teacher is not looking.

How would you feel?

What would you do?

Situation 7

An older student teases a member of your group all the time and says she will hurt you if you tell the teacher.

How would you feel?

What would you do?

Situation 8

A group of students has taken over an area at school that it says is only for them. The students threaten you and your friends each time you come near that area.

How would you feel?

What would you do?

Name: _____

Character Study

A Bug's Life

Characters	Ringleader	Bullied	Contributor	Supporter
Hopper	✓			
Other grasshoppers				
Flik		✓		
Queen		✓		✓
Princess Atta				✓
Dot				
Circus bugs				

TV show or movie: _____

Characters	Ringleader	Bullied	Contributor	Supporter

Name: _____

Choices and Consequences A

What is the situation?

At recess, you notice an older student playing soccer with a group of elementary school students. The older student is much bigger than the other students and always has the ball. The older student constantly yells at the younger students, telling them off and calling them things like *stupid* and *useless*. You can see the younger students are not happy or enjoying the game.

Plan—What could I do?   What might happen?

| Choice 1 | + |
| | − |

| Choice 2 | + |
| | − |

| Choice 3 | + |
| | − |

| Decision |

Name: _____

A Family Story

Talk to someone in your family about a bullying situation he or she experienced or saw as a child, or describe a bullying situation you might have seen. Together, use your action plan to think about the situation and decide what actions could have been taken to safely help stop the bullying.

Situation
Action
Why this action?
What do you think would have happened next?
What would you do if your first action failed?

Name: _____

The Friendship Shuffle

Situation 1 Your teacher sits a new student in the school next to you. *What can you say?*	**Situation 2** New people move in next door, and you notice they have a child about your age. *How can you meet her?*	**Situation 3** You always seem to be standing near the same boy every morning waiting for the school bus. You would like to make friends with him. *How can you start up a conversation?*
Situation 4 A student in your class lends you a pencil when yours breaks. You want to let him know that you appreciate it. *What can you say?*	**Situation 5** A member of your basketball team is trying very hard but not being very successful in helping your team win. *How can you encourage him?*	**Situation 6** When you play online games with your friend, you usually beat him. However, your friend has just beaten you. *How can you show him that even though you lost, you still enjoyed the game?*
Situation 7 At lunchtime, there is a regular group of students who play basketball. You really enjoy playing basketball too. *How can you join in?*	**Situation 8** You are new at school, and another student is asked by the teacher to give you a tour. *What could you talk about as you are having the tour?*	**Situation 9** You are visiting the arcade and want to play air hockey; however, you don't have anyone to play against. There is a single player next to you. *What can you say to ask him to play a game with you?*
Situation 10 You are playing beach volleyball and need an extra player. There are some kids about your age who are swimming. *How can you ask them to join in?*	**Situation 11** You would like to start up a school band. *What are some ways you could try to recruit people?*	**Situation 12** In your online chat room, someone mentions that he lives in the same area as you. *What could you talk about?*
Situation 13 At school, some kids you don't know are talking about your favorite online game. It is clear they like playing it too. *How could you join in the conversation?*	**Situation 14** Your ideas . . .	**Situation 15** Your ideas . . .

Name: _____

Manners

Situation 1 A new student sits in the seat by the window where you always sit. *What don't you do?* *What can you try?*	**Situation 2** You are staying the night at a friend's house. Her family makes minestrone soup for dinner. You hate minestrone soup. *What don't you do?* *What can you try?*
Situation 3 In art class, you spill paint all over the desk, but nobody—including the teacher—notices. *What don't you do?* *What can you try?*	**Situation 4** You have a group assignment due in three days. You have finished everything you need to do, but your groupmates haven't done any work yet. *What don't you do?* *What can you try?*
Situation 5 At school you are in the computer lab on the Internet when you're supposed to be doing work. You accidentally open a site that infects the computer with a virus. *What don't you do?* *What can you try?*	**Situation 6** Your friend asks to borrow your cell phone after school. Your parents bought you the phone and told you to only use it in emergencies. *What don't you do?* *What can you try?*
Situation 7 At the school dance, another student asks you to dance with him. You don't want to dance. *What don't you do?* *What can you try?*	**Situation 8** You are allowed to invite ten good friends to your party. You are approached by a friend who wants to come but wasn't invited. *What don't you do?* *What can you try?*

Name:

Risk-o-Meter

Students can color this Risk-o-Meter.

Very low	: Light green	High	: Light orange
Low	: Light blue	Very high	: Dark orange
Moderate	: Yellow	Extreme	: Red

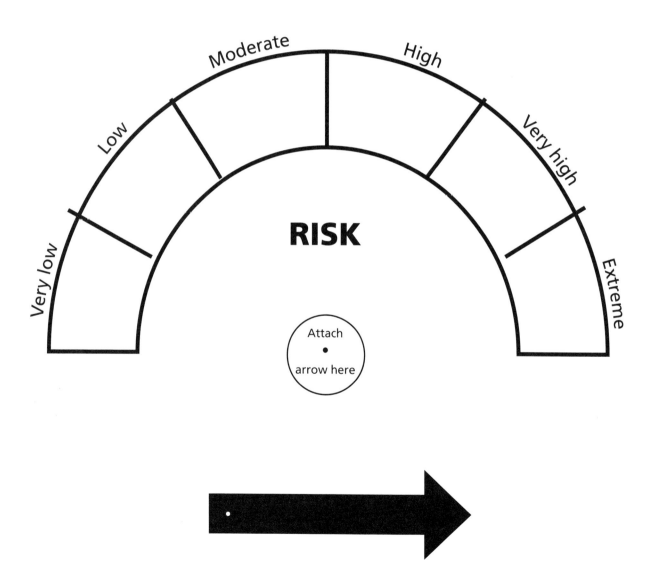

Name: _____

Standing Up for Your Beliefs

Situation 1 You are in the lunchroom and see an older boy take a packet of lollipops and slip it into his jacket pocket. He tries to leave without paying. *How do you feel?* *What do you do?*	**Situation 2** At your math test, the student sitting next to you asks to look at your answers. *How do you feel?* *What do you do?*
Situation 3 At recess, a young student gets the last soccer ball. You see an older student approach him and try to take the ball away. *How do you feel?* *What do you do?*	**Situation 4** Your group is playing a game, and there is no restriction on the number of players. Another student asks to join in the game, but your friends say you already have too many players. *How do you feel?* *What do you do?*
Situation 5 While you are walking to the bus stop with your friends, one of them says she thinks it would be fun to throw garbage at cars driving past. *How do you feel?* *What do you do?*	**Situation 6** There is a long line in the lunchroom. You have been waiting for some time when another student tries to cut in line ahead of you. *How do you feel?* *What do you do?*
Situation 7 You are in the computer labs working on a group assignment. The assignment is due tomorrow, and you aren't finished. The rest of your group starts looking up inappropriate information on the Internet. *How do you feel?* *What do you do?*	**Situation 8** For a treat, your teacher brings in board games to play. There are not enough games for everyone to play, so the class must take turns. One group has played the same game three times in a row and refuses to let anyone else have a turn. *How do you feel?* *What do you do?*

Name: _____

What Do I Do?

The Situation	I Feel, I Think	I Should Not	I Should
You are telling a story to your friends when another student interrupts you and starts telling her own story.			
You're playing doubles table tennis at lunch. Your partner is very bad and keeps missing the ball.			
You have a sleepover with friends on the weekend. One of your friends says he can't come, and you find out later that he went to the movies with some other students.			
At lunch, you are rushing to get in line and another student steps on the back of your shoe. It was an accident, but she doesn't apologize.			
Every day for the whole week, a friend of yours has asked to borrow money from you to buy food at lunch.			

Name: _____

What Goes On Here?

Types of Bullying Behavior	Every Day	Quite Often	Every Now and Then	Hardly Ever	Never
Calling someone names					
Teasing someone about how he or she looks					
Not letting someone join a group					
Sending nasty text messages					
Making fun of other people on social networking sites, like Facebook					
Physically hurting someone					
Telling secrets about someone to others to hurt him or her					
Trying to break up a friendship to hurt someone					
Making someone feel afraid by threatening him or her					
Using threats to keep friendships: "If you don't do this, I won't be your friend."					
Deliberately destroying, damaging, or stealing someone's things					
Sending nasty or threatening messages while chatting on the Internet, such as through Gchat or a chat room					
Deliberately ignoring or leaving someone out of things over the Internet					
Using someone's screen name or password to hurt him or her					
Posting nasty or threatening comments or messages on social networking sites or other websites, like Myspace or Facebook					
Posting unkind pictures or video clips on websites to embarrass, hurt, or upset someone, like on Myspace, YouTube, or a blog					

- What do you think is the most common type of bullying at your school? _____

_____

- What can you do to help stop this type of bullying? _____

_____

- Who can you go to for help to stop bullying in your school? _____

_____

Appendix B: Resource Sheets

Name: _____

Choices and Consequences B

What Is the Situation?

Jane is on her front lawn at home, and her friend says to her, "Look, there's that kid on the roller blades again; let's go and chase her and push her off."

Choice 1

 I could go along with my friend.

Choice 2

 I could suggest we do something else.

Choice 3

 I could say, "I don't want to bully that kid or cause her to be hurt."

Consequences 1

 Good

I do what my friend wants so she will still like me.

 Not So Good

The kid on the roller blades might get hurt.

I might get into trouble for bullying the kid on the roller blades.

Consequences 2

 Good

 My friend will still like me.

The kid on roller blades won't get bullied.

 Not So Good

My friend might still want me to go and bully the kid on roller blades.

Consequences 3

 Good

I won't be bullying.

I won't hurt anyone.

I won't get into trouble.

I will say how I really feel.

 Not So Good

My friend might not like me anymore.

 **Decision**

I will try choice 2 and suggest we do something else first, and if he or she still wants to bully the kid on roller blades, I will try choice 3 and say I don't want to be involved in bullying.

Name: _____

Conflict Situations

Situation 1

A new girl arrives in your class. The teacher asks for one girl to show her around the school. You and two other girls want to be the one to help.

Situation 2

A toy is found and put in the Lost and Found basket. Two students both claim it belongs to them.

Situation 3

At recess, you and three classmates are playing a card game. You have always played the game with the rule that aces are low. One of your classmates says he always plays with the rule that aces are high.

Situation 4

A group of friends is throwing a ball around. The ball goes astray and bounces into the playground. Another student snatches it and won't give it back.

Situation 5

There is only one t-ball set in the sports shed. At recess, you and your friends and another boy and his friends race to get it as soon as the bell goes off. You get the bat, and he gets the stand.

Situation 6

You and another student in the class both get the highest grade in a math test. You get to choose a prize each from the teacher's bag. You both choose the same prize, but she has only one of the items you both want.

Situation 7

At recess, you are working in the library on a group assignment. You have organized to meet your group there, but only one student turns up. The others are all playing basketball instead.

Situation 8

You have a class in the computer lab. There are twenty computers and twenty-one students. You and another student have to share the last computer. You both want to use it for different tasks.

Name: _____

Decision-Making Model

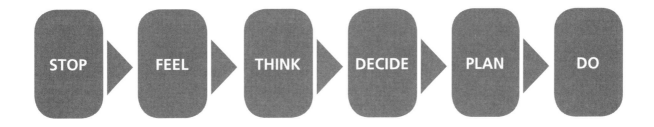

STOP: Assess what is happening. Is it bullying?

FEEL: How do I feel about what is happening?

THINK: Do I think I need to do something about this? Do I need to ask for help?

DECIDE: What choices do I have, and what might the consequences of these choices be?

PLAN: Work out the safest, most effective way to proceed.

DO: Carry out the plan safely.

Name: _____

Feelings Charades

Feeling: Exhausted **Body language**: Slumped posture, droopy eyes, and nodding head **Voice**: Strained, and yawning	**Feeling**: Angry **Body language**: Furrowed brow, arms folded, and scowling **Voice**: Curt, aggressive
Feeling: Confident **Body language**: Chin up, back straight, and smiling **Voice**: Strong, casual	**Feeling**: Distracted **Body language**: Jerky movements, and darting eyes **Voice**: Uhmm, and ahhh
Feeling: Nervous **Body language**: Biting nails, fidgeting, and looking at feet **Voice**: Shaky	**Feeling**: Upset **Body language**: Withdrawn, hands clasped, and frowning **Voice**: Quiet
Feeling: Stressed **Body language**: Rubbing face, blinking, and frowning **Voice**: Tense	**Feeling**: Excited **Body language**: Jittery, grinning, and hyperactive **Voice**: Gleeful

Name: _____

Friendship Firsts

Make the First Move Try being the one to smile first or start a conversation. It is sometimes hard; however, the person you are smiling at might feel just as nervous as you and will appreciate the effort you have made to introduce yourself.	**Join In** Look for places where you can be part of a group. It might be clubs, at your school, sporting clubs, or a place in your community that is looking for students to lend a hand on a volunteer basis.
Show You Care Practice being an active listener. Display a genuine interest in what someone else is telling you. Ask questions about what he or she has told you, so that he or she knows you were really listening.	**Accept Differences** Celebrate the differences in all your friends; accept them for who they are, just as you want them to accept you for who you are.
Take a Chance If you feel comfortable, take the opportunity to share something about yourself with another person. It might be about your favorite TV show or sports you prefer to play and watch.	**Exercise Caution** There will always be people who you will want as friends, but something in your head tells you that it is probably not a good idea. Listen to that voice.
Be Yourself Always make sure that you do not pretend to be someone you are not with your friends. Friends appreciate knowing the real you—your thoughts and feelings, as well as your differences.	**Give and Take** It takes two or more to have a friendship. It is not much fun though, if all the effort is put in by one person. Always try to give as much as you get with your friends.
A Kind Word Friends are supposed to be able to say anything to each other; however, the way we say things can really hurt sometimes. Be gentle with your friends, and think before you speak.	**A Tip From You . . .**

Name: _____

How Do I Avoid Bullying Others?

- Always check that my actions or words are not deliberately hurting someone else's feelings.

- Always check that my actions are not deliberately hurting someone else physically.

- Always check that my actions or words are not deliberately making someone else feel afraid.

- Never try to control someone else or make him or her do something he or she doesn't want to do.

- Never unfairly take out my feelings of anger or frustration on someone else.

- Always ask myself, "Would I like someone else to do this to me?" If the answer is no, then it is a sign to stop my behavior.

Name: _____

"I Could Try . . ." Cards

I could try . . . playing with some of my other friends.

I could try . . . wearing better climbing shoes.

I could try . . . to see it as a great chance to make some new friends as well as keeping my old friends.

I could try . . . to eat less next time.

I could try . . . suggesting that we have a picnic in our backyard instead.

I could try . . . to make sure I wear shin guards the next time I play soccer.

I could try . . . putting it somewhere to dry and then seeing if there is a way to fit it.

I could try . . . watching less TV.

I could try . . . congratulating the person who got the part and telling myself that I will get a turn at the next assembly.

I could try . . . to take more care when getting out of the car.

I could try . . . talking to an adult and asking him or her for help.

I could try . . . to stop running around the pool.

Name: _____

Is This Bullying?

Situation 1 As he is playing tag at recess, a fourth-grade boy runs past a first-grade girl and knocks her water bottle out of her hand. The first-grade girl is upset, but the fourth-grade boy doesn't notice and keeps running.	**Situation 2** A student in your class teases another classmate each day about his hair. This makes him feel sad and not want to come to school.
Situation 3 A third-grade girl punches another third-grade girl on the arm every time she walks past her in the classroom. The punches are hurting her, and she is frightened of the other girl.	**Situation 4** Two boys playing baseball have an argument over whose turn it is to bat, and they begin to fight. Both boys are equally to blame and shouldn't be fighting.
Situation 5 Students in a group, who were your friends last week, stopped letting you be part of their group this week. They say nasty things about you every time you try to join in, and you don't know why.	**Situation 6** All the students in class have given the nickname Greeny Head to Paul because he swims a lot and his hair is a little green. Paul hates this nickname.
Situation 7 A student you are working on a project with on the computer logs on as you and sends really scary messages to other students in your class.	**Situation 8** A friend is visiting your house and suggests you use your parents' cell phone to call people and call them rude names and then hang up.

Name: _____

Is This Situation Harmful?

Situation 1 You are walking to the playground, and you pass a younger student sitting on the edge of an area where some other students the same age are playing. You notice the student who is sitting alone is looking very sad, and you see one of the other students who is playing point at the student sitting alone, say something to the other students, and laugh.	**Situation 2** You are playing soccer on the playground, and you see a group of older boys teasing another boy from their class. The group you are playing with stops to see what is happening, and you see the group of older boys push the other boy over. Then, you see one of the boys kick the boy on the ground.
Situation 3 Every day when you walk out to recess some of your friends walk behind a boy in your class and copy the way the boy is walking or moving. They copy whatever he does. They try to talk others into doing it too. The boy knows they are doing it and tries to ignore them, but you can tell it upsets him.	**Situation 4** There is a girl in your class who is picking on another girl in the class. The teacher doesn't see what is happening because this always happens when the teacher is not looking. She makes faces and throws little pieces of paper at the other girl and then pretends to cry whenever the girl looks upset. Everyone in the class knows what is going on, but this unkind girl is bigger than anyone else and can be very rough.
Situation 5 You are a member of Club Penguin and start getting messages from someone you don't know. He asks you to tell him personal information about yourself.	**Situation 6** A student in your class gets up from her computer and forgets to log off. Another student sits down and starts working on it. You notice he is looking at sites he should not be on.

Name: _____

New Boy

Jeremy is a big boy, and he loves to play football. His family has moved around a lot because of his dad's job. This means Jeremy has to change schools a lot too.

Jeremy finds it hard making new friends only to leave them again and again.

When Jeremy came to our school I could see that he was a bit sad about changing schools again, and he seemed to be a bit grumpy with everyone on his first day. At recess we all went out to the playground. Jeremy hung back and watched as my friends and I grabbed a football from the sports basket and started to kick. Jeremy just sat on the edge of the field and watched that first day, and we carried on playing.

The next day at lunchtime, Jeremy came out to the playground again. This time as one of my friends, Shaun, ran to catch the ball, Jeremy leapt up and ran to where the ball was coming down. As Shaun caught the ball, Jeremy tackled him and slammed him into the ground face first. Jeremy jumped up with the ball and kicked it as far as he could, then turned his back to us with a big smile on his face. Shaun staggered to his feet, and I could see he was trying not to cry, but I didn't want to say anything because it might embarrass him.

The boys at the other end got the ball back and kicked it down our end again. The game continued for a while but I could see that every time Shaun went for the ball, Jeremy would push him and punch his arms.

As the ball came back another time, Jeremy ran up next to Shaun and blocked him. Jeremy pushed Shaun and he fell down hard.

This time Shaun did cry, and I helped him up and walked him to the recess aide.

Jeremy was called over to the recess aide, and we were all asked to explain what had happened. Shaun wasn't the sort of person to try to get others into trouble, but he was clearly upset. He explained to the teacher that Jeremy was being way too rough and was picking on him. I also said that Jeremy seemed to be picking on Shaun.

We all looked at Jeremy, and I was surprised to see that he had tears in his eyes. He just stood there and said nothing. The recess aide sent Jeremy to the time-out area, and we didn't see him for the rest of lunchtime.

After lunch, Jeremy came back to the class from the office with our teacher, Mr. Brown. Mr. Brown asked all of my football friends and me to come outside the classroom door. Jeremy went inside and sat down to silent reading with the rest of the class.

Mr. Brown explained to us that Jeremy had been to many different schools and didn't get the chance to make good friends before he had to move again. But this time his father had a new job that would allow the family to stay for a few years in one place. Mr. Brown said that Jeremy was a pretty shy boy who didn't really know how to make new friends. He explained that Jeremy loved football and had noticed our group did too. He wanted to join in, and he was hoping that if we thought he was really good at football we would want to be his friend.

Jeremy had watched us play on the first day and noticed that Shaun was a really good player, so Jeremy thought that if he could beat Shaun to the ball and kick it a long way we would all think he was really cool.

It all began to make sense. We had actually become a bit afraid of Jeremy and thought he was bullying because he was big and rough, when all he really wanted was to make friends and play football.

Mr. Brown told us he had explained to Jeremy what he had done wrong and suggested some better (more positive) ways of joining in with us. He said that he had told Jeremy that he would speak to us and ask us if we would give Jeremy a second chance.

We all looked at each other and then at Shaun, because he had been the one getting hurt. Shaun smiled and said, "I'm willing to give him a chance if you are," and we all agreed.

As we walked back into the classroom, we all walked past Jeremy's desk, and he looked up at us nervously. As Shaun walked by, he patted Jeremy on the shoulder and said, "See you out at football tomorrow?"

Jeremy looked so relieved, and he smiled and said quietly, "Yes, please, and I promise I will play by your rules."

So it just goes to show, sometimes you have to get to know someone to see what he is really thinking.

Jeremy has been at our school for two years now, and we are all friends. We started playing football on the weekends together. Jeremy and Shaun are our best players and have a great friendship.

Name: _____

Ouch! That Hurts!

You are enjoying a game with friends, and they say you can't play anymore.	You fall out of the tree you are climbing with your brother and injure your arm.
You are placed in a class at the beginning of the year, and all your friends are in the class next door.	You are sick from eating too much food at a party.
You have been promised a picnic in the park, and when the weekend arrives your parents say there is not enough time.	You are accidentally kicked in the leg while playing soccer.
You have nearly finished a painting when someone runs past and spills water all over it.	You have a really bad headache from watching too much TV.
You are not chosen for the part you would like in the class assembly.	You catch your thumb in the car door.
Three students in your class take your lunch every day and laugh at you.	In front of your friends, you slip while running around the pool.

page 1 of 2

Name: _____

✓ Emotional Physical	Emotional ✓ Physical
✓ Emotional Physical	Emotional ✓ Physical
✓ Emotional Physical	Emotional ✓ Physical
✓ Emotional Physical	Emotional ✓ Physical
✓ Emotional Physical	Emotional ✓ Physical
✓ Emotional Physical	Emotional ✓ Physical

Name: _____

A Rainy Day in Shape Town

Name: _____

Shape Town

Once upon a time, there was a beautiful little town called Shape Town built in a valley between two mountains. On one side of the town was a beautiful lake. Many different shapes had lived in the town over the years. All these shapes had some straight sides.

One day, a new shape arrived in town and opened a doughnut shop. The new shape had no straight sides and looked a bit different to all the other shapes in the town (show the "Shapes From Shape Town" resource sheet, and point to the shape at the top of the page). Some of the other shapes began to make fun of the new shape, teasing him because he had no straight edges and was all round. The other shapes in town would not speak to the round shape or go into his shop for doughnuts (show the "Shapes From Shape Town" resource sheet, and point to the two shapes at the bottom of the page). This made the round shape feel very lonely and miserable.

One rainy morning, the round shape went to work and found a sign painted on his shop window, which said, "Go away, we don't need round shapes here." The round shape was so upset that he decided to go home and not even open the shop that day (show the "A Rainy Day in Shape Town" resource sheet, and point to the shape at the top of the page).

The rain continued to pour down on Shape Town and the lake on one side of the town began to swell higher than ever before. The shapes of Shape Town began to panic as they saw the water rising higher and coming closer to their homes. A town meeting was called, and all the shapes were called together in the town hall, except for the round shape. The shapes decided the only way to save their town and their homes was to get together and make a wall between the two mountains to stop the water in the lake from rising until the rain stopped.

All the shapes at the meeting went to the edge of the lake between the mountains and began to form themselves into a wall (show the "A Rainy Day in Shape Town" resource sheet and point to the picture at the bottom of the page).

(Hand out envelopes containing shapes prepared from the "Template for Shape Wall" resource sheet for each group of three to four to try to build the wall to save Shape Town.)

Name: _____

Shapes From Shape Town

Name: _____

Shoe Shuffle

A parent who has just had a really hard day at work and comes home to find the dishes unwashed	A person whose Internet won't work, and he needs to send an urgent message
A student who is selected for the school volleyball team and gets injured just before the pep rally	A person who can't go to a party because he or she is grounded
A person whose mother is very sick	A student who trips on the assembly stage in front of the whole school
A person who is moving to a new school for the first time	A person whose best friend is moving to another school
A person whose best friend has told her she doesn't want to be friends anymore	A person who has his lunch dumped out of his lunchbox every day by another student
A student who is made fun of every time the class goes to physical education	A student who hears that other people are talking about her on Gchat
A student who has found a nasty blog about her created by other students at school	

Name: _____

Situation Cards A

Situation 1 Someone is calling you horrible names almost every day.	**Situation 2** Someone hits or kicks you whenever she sees you.
Situation 3 Each morning, a group of students threatens to hurt you if you don't give the students your lunch money.	**Situation 4** Some students turn their backs on you and ignore you every time you try to talk to them.
Situation 5 A student has been telling awful, untrue stories about you to turn your friends against you.	**Situation 6** A student keeps taking your pencils and breaking them in half and then giving them back while the teacher is not looking.
Situation 7 An older student teases you all the time and says he will hurt you if you tell the teacher.	**Situation 8** Students in a group have taken over an area at school that they say is only for them and you can't go there.

Name: _____

Situation Cards B

Situation 1 You see someone throw another student's bag in the mud at the bus stop. You are annoyed because he always does horrible things to this student.	**Situation 2** You see a student your age punching a younger student every time he sees that student on the playground.
Situation 3 During the last week, a couple of the students in your group have not let another student join in your games at recess and lunchtime.	**Situation 4** Another student has tripped your friend on purpose a couple of times on the playground while you are trying to play. It is upsetting your friend.
Situation 5 A person in your class keeps interfering in the game of some younger students by running through the middle and kicking the ball away. They don't know what to do.	**Situation 6** A small group of students keeps emailing another student in your class, calling him names and making comments about his size.

Name: _____

Situation Shuffle: Values

Situation 1

A boy in your class tells the rest of the class that he won the Best and Fairest Award on his local baseball team over the weekend. You know he didn't because your father coaches that team.

How would you feel?
What would you do?

Situation 2

You see your best friend take a brand-new pen out of another student's bag on the hooks outside your classroom. Your friend tells you that he bought it yesterday. You see the other student is very upset because his new pen is missing.

How would you feel?
What would you do?

Situation 3

The student sitting next to you leaves her desk to speak to the teacher. A student from the next desk leans over and scratches the front cover of her borrowed library book with a pin. When the student returns the book to the library, you hear the librarian telling her she will have to pay for the damaged book.

How would you feel?
What would you do?

Situation 4

A student starts making unkind comments about another student's changing body shape.

How would you feel?
What would you do?

Situation 5

There is a new girl in your class, and you would like to get to know her and try to be her friend, however, the other girls in your group have said they do not want any more people in the group.

How would you feel?
What would you do?

Situation 6

Your parents won't let you go online and talk with your friends on Gchat because they say they don't trust you.

How would you feel?
What would you do?

Situation 7

A boy in your class gets into trouble for something you did because he doesn't tell the teacher it was you.

How would you feel?
What would you do?

Situation 8

Your team goes from first place to last when you drop the ball at the school sports day.

How would you feel?
What would you do?

Name: _____

Snakes and Ladders

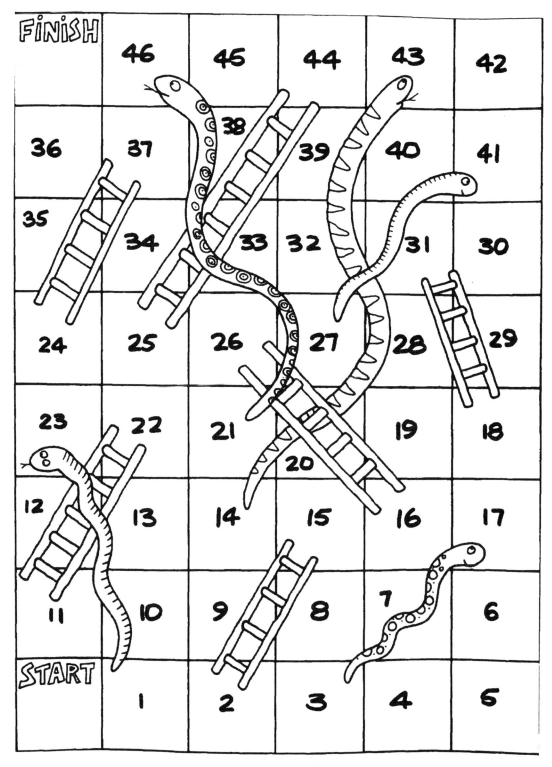

Name:

Sorting Out a Conflict

1. Treat each other with respect; no blaming or put-downs. Talk in quiet, calm voices.

2. Attack the problem, not the person. Think about the problem, and brainstorm solutions.

3. Wait for your turn to speak; no interrupting.

4. Repeat what you think was said to you (this is not agreeing with the person, it is letting him or her know that you understand what he or she is saying and how he or she is feeling).

5. Work together to find a fair solution for both parties, and stick to what you have decided.

6. Present your view of the situation in a truthful way.

7. Talk again if the solution is not working, and then if you can't work it out, ask for help.

Name: _____

Story of Young Wilbur Chapman and His Pig Pete

This story is about how the very first piggy bank came into being.

In 1913, a young boy named Wilbur Chapman lived in Kansas. Around that time, Kansas was mostly made up of ranches and farms. The people did not have a lot of money. They grew grain and raised pigs, chickens, and cows. They didn't have guests very often—especially not guests who could talk about their travels to exciting countries like Mr. Danner could. Mr. Danner was a missionary. A missionary is someone who goes to other places to do charity work to help people in need.

Mr. Danner spoke of the work he had done with his friends in China, Africa, and India who helped men, women, boys, and girls who had leprosy. He had come to Wilbur's house because he was raising money for the people who suffered from leprosy.

Leprosy is a disease that causes sores all over the body, and these sores usually leave horrible scars. Leprosy was quite common many years ago but not much was known about the disease in those days, and people were very frightened of anyone who had leprosy. As time went on, doctors and missionaries learned more about leprosy and how to help people who had it. These days, we see very few cases of the disease.

All afternoon, Mr. Danner told Wilbur and his family stories of boys and girls who were forced to leave home because they had leprosy. He told them about mothers and fathers who had leprosy so badly that they couldn't work or take care of their children. He asked if they would be able to help. Wilbur's mother and father wanted to help. They said they would talk to some of their friends and see if they could raise enough money to help ten people who had leprosy.

Just before Mr. Danner left Wilbur's house, he pulled three shiny silver dollars out of his pocket. "Here you go, Wilbur," he said as he flipped the coins to Wilbur. "Thanks for being such a wonderful host." When Wilbur went to bed that night he prayed that the children and people with leprosy would be safe. Before he fell asleep, he tried to think of what he could do with the silver dollars.

What do you think he could do?

The next morning, he ran downstairs and explained to his mom and dad that he was going to buy a pig with his silver dollars. Now you might think that's kind of an odd thing for a boy to buy, but Wilbur knew that if he took good care of the pig and fed it lots of good food and clean water, it would grow big and fat and he could sell it for a lot more money—like an investment. His parents thought that was a pretty good idea, so his dad went with him to buy a small pig.

Wilbur named his pig Pete. Every morning before school and every afternoon before supper, Wilbur gave Pete a special mixture of corn and grain. Sometimes, on special days, Wilbur fed Pete an apple or scraps from the house. Pete grew fat.

In the meantime, Wilbur's mom was asking all of her friends and neighbors if they would help her raise enough money to help ten people who had leprosy. By autumn, she had raised enough money to help nine. She counted her money over and over again, as if she thought that by magic the extra money would appear.

Wilbur knew if he sold Pete, he would have enough money to add to the collection to help ten people. Wilbur couldn't believe it—the money Mr. Danner had given him had multiplied into enough so that he could help one person with leprosy. Wilbur was pretty excited about his contribution. After all, he was just a kid—he still went to school.

Mr. Danner and other workers in the Leprosy Mission were excited about Wilbur and how his pig was able to help someone with leprosy. They decided they would challenge kids all over America to raise money. They made banks in the shape of a pig and gave them to boys and girls from coast to coast.

These were the very first of the piggy banks that we use today.

Source: Adapted from Leprosy Mission Canada. (n.d.). *Pete the Pig*. Accessed at www.leprosy.ca/Document/Du?id=47 on December 9, 2013.

Name:

Template for Shape Wall

Use this as a template to cut a piece of paper into similar shapes. Make sure you start with the circle in the middle. Put only the shapes with straight sides in the envelopes for the groups.

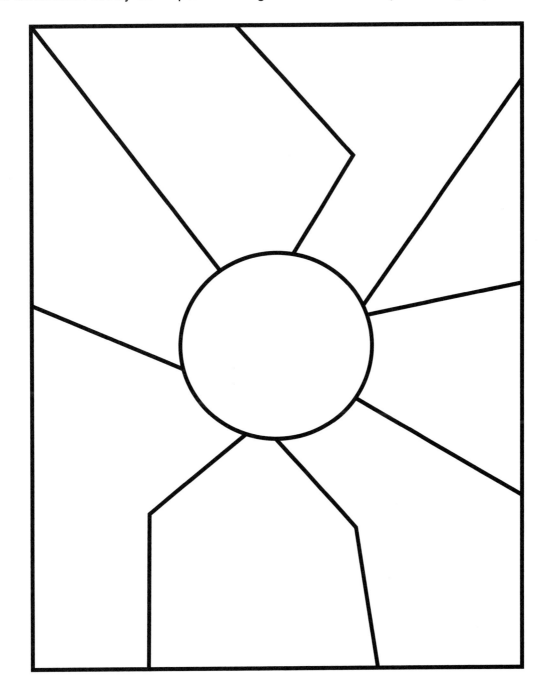

Name: _____

Types of Bullying

Bullying is when any of the following behaviors happen again and again to someone, and it is hard for the person being bullied to stop this from happening. Some types of bullying include:

Exclusion

- Being deliberately ignored, left out on purpose, or not allowed to join in

Physical

- Being deliberately hit, kicked, or pushed around

Lies or Rumors

- Having lies or nasty stories told about someone to make other kids not like him or her

Threats

- Being made afraid of getting hurt
- Staring or giving someone mean looks or gestures
- Forcing someone to do things he or she doesn't want to

Verbal Abuse and Teasing

- Deliberately being made fun of and teased in a mean and hurtful way

Cyber

- Deliberately being hurt online or by phone (such as when using a social networking site like Club Penguin)

> **Bullying is used by a more powerful person to cause fear, distress, or other harm to a less powerful person who is unable to stop the bullying from happening.**

Name: _____

What Is Bullying?

Bullying is when one or more of the following things happen again and again to someone who finds it hard to stop it from happening again. Bullying is when a person or a group of people offline or online (cell phone or Internet):

Make fun of and tease someone in a mean and hurtful way

Tell lies or spread nasty rumors about someone to try to make others not like him or her

Leave someone out on purpose or not allow them to join in

Hit, kick, or push someone around

Deliberately damage, destroy, or steal someone's things

Threaten or make someone feel afraid of getting hurt

It is *not* bullying when:

Teasing is done in a friendly, playful way

Two people who are as strong as each other argue or fight

Cyberbullying—using, for example, a cell phone or the Internet—is when a person:

- Sends nasty or threatening emails or messages on the Internet or via cell phone
- Sends mean or nasty comments or pictures about others to websites like Myspace, Facebook, or Gchat or to other students' cell phones
- Deliberately ignores or leaves others out over the Internet
- Pretends to be someone else online to hurt someone or make him or her look foolish

Cyberbullying can happen when things such as hurtful text messages, pictures, video clips, and emails are being sent to you. It can also happen when these things are sent to others about you.

Name: _____

When It's OK to Say "No"

An older student emails you at your school email address asking you for your lunch money.	A girl who is not part of your group emails you an invitation to her birthday party. You don't want to go, but you don't want to hurt her feelings.
Your friend writes you a note asking you to meet him at the local playground after school.	A stranger asks you to get in his car.
Your best friend brings some matches to school and asks you to burn some leaves with her.	The bus driver asks to see your ticket.
Another student picks on you, and a group forms around both of you. Students chant "fight, fight, fight." You do not want to look afraid in front of your friends.	In your group of friends, one student wants to skip school for the day. All of your other friends say "yes."

References and Resources

Anderson, D. K., Reher, K. (Producers), & Lasseter, J. (Director). (1998). *A bug's life* [motion picture]. United States: Walt Disney Pictures.

Baldry, A. C., & Farrington, D. P. (2007). Effectiveness of programs to prevent school bullying. *Victims & Offenders, 2*(2), 183–204.

Banks, L. R. (2001). *The Indian in the cupboard*. London: HarperCollins Children's.

Blabey, A. (2007). *Pearl Barley and Charlie Parsley*. Camberwell, Victoria, Australia: Penguin.

Brendgen, M., Markiewicz, D., Doyle, A. B., & Bukowski, W. M. (2001). The relations between friendship quality, ranked-friendship preference, and adolescents' behavior with their friends. *Merrill-Palmer Quarterly, 47*(3), 395–415.

Brodmann, A. (1998). *The gift: A Hanukkah story*. New York: Aladdin.

Buzan, T. (2003). *Mind maps for kids: An introduction*. London: HarperCollins.

Child Health Promotion Research Centre. (2010). *An empirical intervention to reduce cyber-bullying in adolescents: Annual report to Healthway*. Perth, Western Australia, Australia: Author.

Collaborative for Academic, Social, and Emotional Learning. (2003). *Safe and sound: An educational leader's guide to evidence-based social and emotional learning (SEL) programs*. Chicago: Author.

Collaborative for Academic, Social, and Emotional Learning. (2011). *Illinois Social Emotional Learning Standards*. Accessed at http://casel.org/wp-content/uploads/2011/04/Illinois-SEL-Standards.pdf on January 2, 2014.

Cook, J. (2006). *My mouth is a volcano!* Chattanooga, TN: National Center for Youth Issues.

Coulman, V. (2001). *When pigs fly*. Montreal, Quebec, Canada: Lobster Press.

Craig, W. M., Pepler, D., & Atlas, R. (2000). Observations of bullying in the playground and in the classroom. *School Psychology International, 21*(1), 22–36.

Craig, W. M., Pepler, D. J., & Blais, J. (2007). Responding to bullying: What works? *International Journal of School Psychology, 28*(4), 15–24.

Crick, N. R., & Bigbee, M. A. (1998). Relational and overt forms of peer victimization: A multiinformant approach. *Journal of Consulting and Clinical Psychology, 66*(2), 337–347.

Crick, N. R., & Dodge, K. A. (1994). A review and reformulation of social information-processing mechanisms in children's adjustment. *Psychological Bulletin, 115*(1), 74–101.

Cross, D., Shaw, T., Hearn, L., Epstein, M., Monks, H., Lester, L., et al. (2009). *Australian covert bullying prevalence study (ACBPS)*. Perth, Western Australia, Australia: Child Health Promotion Research Centre, Edith Cowan University.

Dasent, G. W. (1859). *Popular tales from the Norse*. New York: Appleton.

Dodge, K. A., & Coie, J. D. (1987). Social-information-processing factors in reactive and proactive aggression in children's peer groups. *Journal of Personality and Social Psychology, 53*(6), 1146–1158.

Dodge, K. A., Lochman, J. E., Harnish, J. D., Bates, J. E., & Pettit, G. S. (1997). Reactive and proactive aggression in school children and psychiatrically impaired chronically assaultive youth. *Journal of Abnormal Psychology, 106*(1), 37–51.

Dooley, J. J., Cross, D., Hearn, L., & Treyvaud, R. (2009). *Review of existing Australian and international cyber-safety research*. Perth, Western Australia, Australia: Child Health Promotion Research Centre, Edith Cowan University.

Elkind + Sweet Communications. (n.d.). *How to cope with an unpleasant feeling*. Accessed at www.goodcharacter.com/YCC/Feelings.html on December 10, 2013.

Elman, N. M., & Kennedy-Moore, E. (2003). *The unwritten rules of friendship*. Boston: Little, Brown.

Emmer, E. T., & Stough, L. M. (2001). Classroom management: A critical part of educational psychology, with implications for teacher education. *Educational Psychologist, 36*(2), 103–112.

Farrington, D. P., & Ttofi, M. M. (2009). School-based programs to reduce bullying and victimization. *Campbell Systematic Reviews, 6*. Oslo, Norway: Campbell Collaboration.

Fontaine, R. G., & Dodge, K. A. (2006). Real-time decision making and aggressive behavior in youth: A heuristic model of response evaluation and decision (RED). *Aggressive Behavior, 32*(6), 604–624.

Fox, M. (2009). *Wilfrid Gordon McDonald Partridge*. Parkside, South Australia, Australia: Omnibus Books.

Galen, B. R., & Underwood, M. K. (1997). A developmental investigation of social aggression among children. *Developmental Psychology, 33*(4), 589–600.

Halliwell, J. O. (1886). *The nursery rhymes of England*. London: Warne.

Hume, L. (2007). *Clancy the courageous cow*. Parkside, South Australia, Australia: Omnibus Books.

Humphrey, S. M. (2007). *Hot issues, cool choices*. Amherst, NY: Prometheus Books.

International Union for Health Promotion and Education. (n.d.). *Achieving health promoting schools: Guidelines for promoting health in schools, version 2*. Saint-Denis, France: Author.

Korman, J., & Fontes, R. (1998). *A bug's life*. New York: Disney Press.

Lagerspetz, K., Björkqvist, K., & Peltonen, T. (1988). Is indirect aggression typical of females? Gender differences in aggressiveness in 11- to 12-year-old children. *Aggressive Behavior, 14*(6), 403–414.

Leprosy Mission Canada. (n.d.). *Pete the pig*. Accessed at www.leprosy.ca/Document.Doc?id=47 on December 9, 2013.

Ludwig, T. (2005). *My secret bully*. Berkeley, CA: Tricycle Press.

McCain, B. R. (2001). *Nobody knew what to do: A story about bullying*. Morton Grove, IL: Whitman.

McNeely, C. A., Nonnemaker, J. M., & Blum, R. W. (2002). Promoting school connectedness: Evidence from the National Longitudinal Study of Adolescent Health. *Journal of School Health, 72*(4), 138.

Moroney, T. (2007). *When I'm feeling jealous*. Scoresby, Victoria, Australia: Five Mile Press.

Munson, D. (2000). *Enemy pie*. San Francisco: Chronicle Books.

Naylor, P. R. (1994). *King of the playground*. New York: Atheneum Books.

O'Connell, P., Pepler, D., & Craig, W. (1999). Peer involvement in bullying: Insights and challenges for intervention. *Journal of Adolescence, 22*(4), 437–452.

Olweus, D. (1996). *The revised Olweus bully/victim questionnaire*. Bergen, Norway: Research Centre for Health Promotion, University of Bergen.

O'Neill, A. (2002). *The recess queen*. New York: Scholastic.

Piper, W. (1990). *The little engine that could* (60th anniv. ed.). New York: Platt & Munk.

Rigby, K. (1996). *Bullying in schools and what to do about it*. Melbourne, Victoria, Australia: ACER Press.

Sierra, J. (2007). *Mind your manners, B.B. Wolf*. New York: Knopf.

Smith, J. D., Schneider, B. H., Smith, P. K., & Ananaidou, K. (2004). The effectiveness of whole-school antibullying programs: A synthesis of evaluation research. *School Psychology Review, 33*(4), 547–560.

Smith, P. K., Talamelli, L., Cowie, H., Naylor, P., & Chauhan, P. (2004). Profiles of non-victims, escaped victims, continuing victims and new victims of school bullying. *British Journal of Educational Psychology, 74*(4), 565–582.

Smokowski, P. R., & Holland, K. (2005). Bullying in school: Correlates, consequences, and intervention strategies for school social workers. *Children & Schools, 27*(2), 101–110.

Thiele, C. (2004). *Storm boy*. Sydney, New South Wales, Australia: New Holland.

Thompson, C. (2009). *The big little book of happy sadness*. North Sydney, New South Wales, Australia: Random House.

Viorst, J. (1987). *Alexander and the terrible, horrible, no good, very bad day*. New York: Aladdin.

Vitiello, B., & Stoff, D. M. (1997). Subtypes of aggression and their relevance to child psychiatry. *Journal of the American Academy of Child and Adolescent Psychiatry, 36*(3), 307–315.

Vreeman, R. C., & Carroll, A. E. (2007). A systematic review of school-based interventions to prevent bullying. *Archives of Pediatric and Adolescent Medicine, 161*(1), 78–88.

Friendly Schools Plus Series Set

The Friendly Schools Plus series by Donna Cross, Shane Thompson, and Erin Erceg uses an evidence-based, whole-school approach to reduce bullying and to foster a supportive school culture. This approach recognizes that all aspects of students' school life influence their academic performance and health. The seven Friendly Schools Plus resources provide educators with tools to create effective programs that support students academically and socially, help students practice healthy interpersonal behaviors in school and online, and encourage parental and stakeholder school involvement.

KTB001

The seven books in the *Friendly Schools Plus* series
by Donna Cross, Shane Thompson, and Erin Erceg

Friendly Schools Plus Teacher Resource: Early Childhood (Ages 4–6)
BKB001

Friendly Schools Plus Teacher Resource: Early & Middle Adolescence (Ages 11–14)
BKB005

Friendly Schools Plus Teacher Resource: Early Childhood (Ages 6–8)
BKB002

Friendly Schools Plus Evidence for Practice: Whole-School Strategies to Enhance Students' Social Skills and Reduce Bullying in Schools
BKB006

Friendly Schools Plus Teacher Resource: Middle Childhood (Ages 8–10)
BKB003

Friendly Schools Plus Friendly Families
BKB007

Friendly Schools Plus Teacher Resource: Middle Childhood (Ages 10–11)
BKB004